SEVEN SECRET POWERS OF LOVE
(Ninth Graders' Dream Primer For Smoke-Free Thriving Lives)

Humbler Acts

Humbler Acts

SEVEN SECRET POWERS OF LOVE

(NINTH GRADERS' DREAM PRIMER FOR SMOKE-FREE THRIVING LIVES)

COPYRIGHT HUMBLER ACTS MMXVI

Copyright© 2016 by Humbler Acts

All rights reserved. No part of this book may be reproduced in any form or by any electronic or mechanical means, including information storage and retrieval systems, without permission in writing from the author:

Humbler Acts at e-mail address, humbleracts@aol.com.

ISBN 978-0-9717186-1-6

CONTENTS

Dedication	[i]
Preface	[ii]
Foreword	[iv]
Day #1—Monday—The Instinctive Force	[1]
Day #2—Tuesday—The Sexual Force	[3]
Day #3—Wednesday—The Moving Force	[7]
Day #4—Thursday—The Feeling Force	[9]
Day #5—Friday—The Thinking Force	[12]
Day #6—Saturday—The Higher Feeling Force	[14]
Day #7—Sunday—The Higher Thinking Force	[16]
Day #8—Monday—The Instinctive Force	[22]
Day #9—Tuesday—The Sexual Force	[24]
Day #10—Wednesday—The Moving Force	[27]
Day #11—Thursday—The Feeling Force	[30]
Day #12—Friday—The Thinking Force	[34]
Day #13—Saturday—The Higher Feeling Force	[37]
Day #14—Sunday—The Higher Thinking Force	[40]
Day #15—Monday—The Instinctive Force	[44]
Day #16—Tuesday—The Sexual Force	[48]
Day #17—Wednesday—The Moving Force	[51]
Day #18—Thursday—The Feeling Force	[56]
Day #19—Friday—The Thinking Force	[62]
Day #20—Saturday—The Higher Feeling Force	[69]
Day #21—Sunday—The Higher Thinking Force	[72]
Day #22—Monday—The Instinctive Force	[75]
Day #23—Tuesday—The Sexual Force	[77]
Day #24—Wednesday—The Moving Force	[81]
Day #25—Thursday—The Feeling Force	[84]
Day #26—Friday—The Thinking Force	[88]
Day #27—Saturday—The Higher Feeling Force	[93]
Day #28—Sunday—The Higher Thinking Force	[99]
Day #29—Monday—The Instinctive Force	[103]
Day #30—Tuesday—The Sexual Force	[108]

CONTENTS (CON'T.)

Day #31—Wednesday—The Moving Force [113]
Day #32—Thursday—The Feeling Force [116]
Day #33—Friday—The Thinking Force [120]
Day #34—Saturday—The Higher Feeling Force [124]
Day #35—Sunday—The Higher Thinking Force [129]
Day #36—Monday—The Instinctive Force [133]
Day #37—Tuesday—The Sexual Force [137]
Day #38—Wednesday—The Moving Force [140]
Day #39—Thursday—The Feeling Force [143]
Day #40—Friday—The Thinking Force [146]
Day #41—Saturday—The Higher Feeling Force [150]
Day #42—Sunday—The Higher Thinking Force [157]
Day #43—Monday—The Instinctive Force [162]
Day #44—Tuesday—The Sexual Force [165]
Day #45—Wednesday—The Moving Force [169]
Day #46—Thursday—The Feeling Force [173]
Day #47—Friday—The Thinking Force [178]
Day #48—Saturday—The Higher Feeling Force [182]
Day #49—Sunday—The Higher Thinking Force [189]
Day #50—Monday—The Instinctive Force (Jubilee) [194]

*I dedicate this book
To all of the young men
And women who
Are ninth graders—*

*Who may feel lost in a
World without direction…*

*May this earnest
Primer be a
Source of guidance and hope
For navigating their
Lives and helping them steer
In the right paths
Of truth and love…*

*May their lives be enriched
With the knowledge dreams hold,
And may they serve
Mankind always.*

PREFACE

I've built this book to help all ninth graders (from all backgrounds) steer clear of tobacco and learn from their own dreams to strive to be thriving.

At the age where ninth graders are, they are quite possibly not involved in smoking and have a choice to avoid it.

Yet, my purpose building this book is not only to keep you from those cigarettes but also to teach you a unique way to dream for a purpose that leads you to make your life a thriving one like you've never known. I know you may doubt me now, but I am going to give you a way to avoid smoking and (with the same system) show how to use your dreams to strive to be thriving.

By "thriving" I mean to point to how you as a young friend can learn from your own dreams all the unknown richness that you can have in your young life. I firmly believe that if you follow what I teach you—and have faith and kindness towards your abilities—you can wind up with an expo of experiences that will benefit you.

So stay with me as I start out. First, let me affirm that—despite what life now holds—(rephrasing a by-gone singer) "YOU AIN'T LIVED NUTHIN' YET!" In other words, so far as your own life and what you think of how it is going—and what you have witnessed—you cannot yet imagine how amazing are the gems you may discover with regard to your unwitnessed worth.

It doesn't matter (as far as I am concerned) whether you've been born with bad stuff or whether you've been blessed with the best of good stuff, within you there stands unknown stuff that can transform you from young mundane thoughts to bold astonishing revelations.

These revelations will be all-thriving for you—and grant you a sense of freedom that heralds happiness. Again, I say, you will find a range of revelations which will help you live a life that's filled with thriving.

This isn't to guarantee you'll be rich, famous and be loved by all whom you meet. Miracles might happen to you—but my own down-to-earth hope is that you'll begin to have dream-gifts that will guide you towards living a life that is thriving in every way.

So I'd rather envision your thoughts, feelings and other parts of you becoming more harmonized; and as your state of harmony is glimpsed, folks begin to take note that you possess "the full value" that's recognizable in a special person.

FOREWORD

If you learn little else --as we share this primer--I wish you'd grasp the prime premise: the purpose of dreams (as far as I am concerned) is to improve Forces in you. Let me state that again: the purpose of dreams is to improve your Forces within. It's paramount that you impress that on your mind. Upon the prime premise rests this whole dream primer that will shortly benefit you.

Let's continue to learn some more.

...I have mentioned Forces. Just what are these Forces? In you there are Seven Forces. Maybe you've guessed a few before I reveal them:

(1.) the Instinctive Force
(2.) the Sexual Force
(3.) the Moving Force
(4.) the Feeling Force
(5.) the Thinking Force
(6.) the Higher Feeling Force
(7.) the Higher Thinking Force

Now let's further reflect: the purpose of your dreams is to improve all seven of these Forces. "Why?" You ask, "Is it critical to improve all these Seven Forces?"

Here's the simple answer: in order to be fit enough TO KEEP FROM SMOKING and TO STRIVE TO BE THRIVING, you've got to prime each Force to a measure of harmony –where these herein-mentioned goals can surely be met. It's like getting ready to scale a tall peak. Every part of you must be in shape. Otherwise your journey is jinxed.

I wish you to succeed; I wish you to be strong in your Seven Forces so that by this primer's finish you will be convinced that you're ready to resist smoking and strive to be thriving.

In the beginning, though, you may doubt that dreams will help you. But you'll find dreams can help; dreams just have to sense that you are earnest in your efforts.

...So far I've talked to you about two ideas. One: your dreams will help improve each of your Seven Forces. Two: I've told you what those Seven Forces actually are.

Now in order to plot a simple meaningful progression of these Forces, we need to link them to a manageable framework. Happily for us there are already seven days in a week... The following shows how all the Seven Forces are connected to the seven days of the week:

the Instinctive Force: Monday
the Sexual Force: Tuesday
the Moving Force: Wednesday
the Feeling Force: Thursday
the Thinking Force: Friday
the Higher Feeling Force: Saturday
the Higher Thinking Force: Sunday

Am I going too fast? Are you starting to ask: "What have I got myself into?"

Well, the last thing I want to happen is: lose you.

So let's see if I can backtrack and then slowly come forth with some new assistance.

I've been talking about how your dreams possess a purpose to help improve your days—notwithstanding others' theories-- by helping to improve the Seven Forces—the entirety of your being.

...Everything you think, feel do or exist upon is tied into all these Forces.

So the goals that I've set for you to accomplish can't be reached till all your Forces have been given a chance to develop from dreams.

Yes, I know that's got to sound strange, but on that premise the value of this book rests.

Now as we get ready to start on your dreaming, I wish to give you several tips that will help prepare you for eventual success. (I've gone all out for you!)

But before the tips, let me say: I have dedicated myself to fifty days of dreaming, just as you will do. (Or at least that's my hope!)

Before you get in bed, you should look at the two tip sheets, which I would like to go over with you right now. (Find them after these four pages.)

Now follow me as I stretch for your attention.

Detach those two pages from the book while I now explain all of the thoughts expressed.

They're detached ? Good!

Let us begin.

The first sheet shows you the format to read over before you get in bed. As you can see, the sheet affirms the two goals that you have:

(1.) To be smoke-free
(2.) And strive to be thriving.

Are you with me on this?

Next you will take note of a number (Day #1) and then Monday...

What is this all about?

Each of the fifty days is numbered— and each Force is shown next to day and number— starting with Instinctive Force and going to and ending with the Instinctive Force on the last day--#50.

Next on this same tip sheet you will find a strong statement that is necessary to note: IMPROVE YOUR INSTINCTIVE FORCE THROUGH DREAMS—TO ACHIEVE YOUR GOALS!

You will find such a statement on each of the fifty tip sheets that precede each of the fifty sections that have the dreams I've done for you.

This is a typical first page that is designed to emphasize your goals each day.

Lastly, on this first page you will see two columns that are there to accommodate the dreams that you jot down upon awakening.

I use this same format to keep track of all that I dream. I use it as follows:

First, I jot down my dreams on the right side of the page where "Jotted-Down Dreams" appear.

Then later in the day, sometime—on the left side--I'll spend time writing up the dreams, so they are more clearly expressed.

Hopefully, as you find yourself needing more space for jotting down and writing up your dreams, you will use your own paper—and copy down the format as I've shown here.

Glance at this sheet each night before getting in bed—so as to keep yourself on track.

Now, let's look over the second page that has the two important questions to ask--after you've written up the dreams that you have had.

You will find that I ask these two questions after every dream that I have shown you. They're drill-queries; and though they may seem tedious or not always necessary, I have found each of them crucial.

Each helps my mind focus and certify the pulse of a dream I may not have sensed.

#1) WHAT'S MY EXPERIENCE WITH THIS DREAM FROM LAST NIGHT?

As you'll find in the dreams I've had, I try my best to write what I've experienced. Then I follow with this question:

#2) HOW DOES THIS DREAM IMPROVE THE FORCE I'M WORKING ON?

Here, again, I try hard to write.

I am often amazed that the mere act of my writing down words produces thoughts and feelings that I was unaware of before.

See if you don't find the same truth.

   *   *   *   *

You have now received the total preparation for beginning this dream primer.

You will find-- after each dream that I've recorded—I use the two-question process to get the most value out of the dreams I've had.

If you follow what I have done, you should be able to a-chieve your own success.

Pick Sunday night as the first dream night that you will start with.

If you adhere to the sequence of days--as I've shown you-- my hope is that you'll be in sync with the process.

   *   *   *   *

…The proof is in the pudding's taste; and let's hope your pudding has a taste that you would never have dreamed would be so good!

   *   *   *   *

I have written this dream primer for ninth graders; and any-thing they'd like me to explain or assist in helping them with, please don't hesitate to reach out to me..

Reaching me is simple in any of these ways:

Email: humbleracts@aol.com

Cell Phone: 314-574-7681

Address: Humbler Acts
900 South Hanley Road /Unit 1-E
Clayton, MO 63105
U.S.A.

YOUR GOALS: TO BE SMOKE-FREE AND STRIVE TO BE THRIVING

DAY#1 MONDAY—THE INSTINCTIVE FORCE

IMPROVE YOUR INSTINCTIVE FORCE THROUGH DREAMS—TO ACHIEVE YOUR GOALS!

WRITTEN UP DREAMS | *JOTTED DOWN DREAMS*

DAILY QUESTIONS TO ASK EACH OF THE DREAMS YOU HAVE:

#1.) WHAT'S MY EXPERIENCE WITH THIS DREAM FROM LAST NIGHT?

#2.) HOW DOES THIS DREAM IMPROVE THE FORCE I'M WORKING ON?

DAY #1—MONDAY—THE INSTINCTIVE FORCE

If you failed to recall one dream during this past night or early morning, do not be discouraged. It may take a few nights until you get yourself set to recall. You see, remembering dreams is something that we all can recall—it is just that for so many years we have gotten into the habit of not remembering—because we've heard that dreams are really "only dreams"—lacking any tangible worth

And when you do not give dreams the respect they need, they simply don't give you any respect in making their messages available. So simply look forward to the next night for another opportunity to write down what you can remember.

At first, you may only recollect a couple words or a short sentence or two. There's nothing wrong with that. Often, just a few words (when you review them when awake) have a meaning or a message that can surprise. I can attest to that often.

For those of you who may have been able to write down what you dreamed—after you're up (and it can be any time during the new day), you should review them and do this: start out each dream review by asking, "What's my experience with this one dream?" And then go over the words you have written down and see what your response might be.

I will show you how I do it when I have a dream or two that I can explain. It so happens that last night I didn't write down any dreams that I hoped to have. You see, even after keeping my dreams for more than fifty years, sometimes I don't recall my dreams either!

Hopefully, tomorrow night I'll dream one or two dreams; and then I will show you how I personally work. The thing I will try to do is look over my dreams, and then try to see what my experience is about them. It will be easier to show you what I do with examples than with just talk. I hope how I do it will encourage you to follow my words with your own words.

Naturally, none of us will have the same dreams. Yet the reason I am doing this myself is to help you accustom yourself to how you can do what I teach.

Once you have written down what your experience is with your dream, you can probe how the dream, itself, might help improve the Force you are working on—the Instinctive Force, this particular night.

One thing I need to mention is that you ought never refrain from writing down what your dream is saying. Sometimes the stuff might be something you'll be embarrassed to write down. You wouldn't want somebody else reading it. I can understand how you might well feel like that. So try to keep your dreams private from anyone else looking over your words. I leave it to you how to make sure you can achieve this.

The truth is: dreams do not hold back on stuff they might tell you. It's helpful if you see dreams as friends who want you to have a life that is thriving—a life that is something you can be quite proud of. And although they may say some things that you won't be too proud of, the end result will be that you'll use them to improve.

I hope you'll begin to regard me as your friend and see that as you trust in dreams, you will begin to see that they are worthy friends.

Always keep in your mind your goals are: keeping from smoking and striving to be quite thriving—really wonderful goals.

YOUR GOALS: TO BE SMOKE-FREE AND STRIVE TO BE THRIVING

DAY#2 TUESDAY—THE SEXUAL FORCE

IMPROVE YOUR SEXUAL FORCE THROUGH DREAMS—TO ACHIEVE YOUR GOALS!

WRITTEN UP DREAMS	*JOTTED DOWN DREAMS*

DAILY QUESTIONS TO ASK EACH OF THE DREAMS YOU HAVE:

#1.) WHAT'S MY EXPERIENCE WITH THIS DREAM FROM LAST NIGHT?

#2.) HOW DOES THIS DREAM IMPROVE THE FORCE I'M WORKING ON?

DAY #2—TUESDAY—THE SEXUAL FORCE

I always sense immense gratitude for the reign of dreams that comes while I'm asleep. The thing that amazes me is once we start to jot down our dreams and then begin to write down just what our experience is and then follow that with how these dreams might be messages to help us improve the Force we're working on— we may become aware of some guiding power that's within us. It's as if there's another will.

The whole thing is a great blessing that we all have— once we start to avail ourselves of the benefits that dreams can bestow on us.(Wait and see if you don't agree.)

Let me go over a couple of dreams I had last night and show you how these dreams gave me some insight that I may not have yet had.

Dream #1:'Something about seeing a thick stone wall and then seeing feelings there behind it.'

Now, remember: this is my dream; and what I try to do is read over it and try to get some sort of experience from it.

I recall the wall—it's quite thick. It's the sort of wall that must have been built to keep something inside from getting out and to keep stuff outside from ever getting in. That's almost a given to me.

Now recall: I said that there were "feelings" behind it. I may not comprehend what feelings are behind it; yet those feelings would not be able to get past the wall.

It strikes me that the wall is so much thicker than those feelings are strong… In other words, whatever feelings are behind that wall are really not so fierce. That wall is an overreaction for keeping those feelings from getting out.

Let's say that's all the time we're spending on the experience part.

Next we need to ask ourselves, 'How does this dream improve the Force we are working on?'

… Which comes down to asking ourselves: 'How is my Sexual Force improved by this dream?" Each of us —if we had this dream—would have to honestly ask ourselves this question. Since it's my dream, I ask myself; and here's what I come up with: I'm almost eighty years' old, and my Sexual Force is undergoing what usually happens to a male my age. Our feelings are still like a young man's, but our sexual power is quite diminished..

It's like a wall keeps our feelings inside because we aren't able to express them through any sex. I mean, we can love our significant other (in my case, my wife of more than fifty-three years)—but we can't get over the wall to put our love into action.

So this dream is simply telling me—and-- in so telling—helping me understand— that I should not decry the situation I'm now in—but see it as a state that I can live with and somehow benefit from

So much anger that people show comes from their not being able to properly deal with their sex-- thanks to their age. As a matter of fact, even young people feel angry because they aren't able to deal with this Force that we are talking about.

A lot of young folks start smoking in order to express their Sexual Force—but expressing it this way only causes an inner grief in their spiritual self. It's subtle but it's truly there.

Now I hope you have got something out of this dream.

There is one more dream to discuss that occurred after I experienced the first:

^   *   *   *

Dream #2: 'My foreman comes in—and I think I overhear him telling a guy he's turning in his resignation. Now he stands there talking about his past performance—and as he goes on, I can't tell whether he's quitting or just getting stuff off his chest. I look at him and see his thick black eyebrows. I'm getting a bit uneasy. If he and his partner quit—I won't really have a fabricating business any more. But maybe that's good. Maybe I am better without that part of the business. I'd still have the plain steel. And I just had a source outside make up some stairs; and I've asked the foreman to check it out to see if the whole set has been made correctly. So on and on the guy--who's my foreman—talks—not yet telling me what he's going to do—though the gist of what he's saying is he got no bonus or pay increase.

Now as I mentioned to you before, the first thing I do is to experience how I feel as this man is venting his problems. One part of me fears he's leaving, and one part says, 'The part of the business he heads up is full of anxious problems.' So you can see, I am in a quandary with what's going to be with his talk.

After I've spent some time pondering his message, I now ask the question: 'How does this dream improve the Force I am now working on?' Recall: it's the Sexual Force. This linking the dream to the Force we're working on is a key to the success that folks achieve.

You see: the way to achieve your goals-- to keep yourself from smoking and strive to be thriving is---in a step-by-step way--to build up each of your Forces. If our Forces are out of harmony, then we have less chance in our goals' pursuit.

When all of our Forces are in harmony—or aware of where they ought to be— then we can avoid the scourge of smoking and strive to be thriving.

So now we go back to this dream which notes nothing about the Force we are working on-- but just may-- in a sort of hidden manner—slyly be giving us straight advice.

As I've mentioned before: I now am at an age when a male is confronted with the fact his Sexual Force may not be the way it once was… He may have been forewarned, but he is not prepared-- so his outlook on sex needs to be tendered with so that he can be content with his lot that age has assigned him.

When I turn to this dream, I begin to see that the foreman (say, the penis?) is telling me that he is quitting fabricating.

"Fabricating" can mean what one makes and can also mean the way that one's lying. He's telling me he just may have to give up on both things: attempting potency and pretending he still can.

He also mentions that he's not had a bonus (stands for boner?); and he's not had a pay increase (able to ejaculate more?).

Without telling the name of this foreman, it happens to convey a meaning like "wisely forego her private ridge".

How does all of this help improve my Sexual Force? It confronts me with what is realistically proper for me to learn: I am losing my foreman's help; yet I can still show the love I have in plain ways. For me, it might be better not to try hard to work my foreman, and wiser to accept that my business can be more thriving if I learn the benefits of age without regret for any loss.

Now I hope you can see how dreams can help us know the best way we can learn to live. I believe that dreams are always meant for our good. They may cause us uneasiness; and surely it is true that we may not exult in what they have to say to us. But like a friend who tells us the way things now are: dreams prepare us for decent change.

I once had a dream that advised me to become a vegan (one who doesn't eat meat, chicken or fish… or anything that might be termed organic). I railed against change to be one for years — but in time became one— and I think for me it's been great — though surely something that I would never have thought about doing-- without that dream.

I hope at the end of this day, you are starting to apprehend a dream's net worth.

YOUR GOALS: TO BE SMOKE-FREE AND STRIVE TO BE THRIVING

DAY#3—WEDNESDAY—THE MOVING FORCE

IMPROVE YOUR MOVING FORCE THROUGH DREAMS—TO ACHIEVE YOUR GOALS!

WRITTEN UP DREAMS	*JOTTED DOWN DREAMS*

DAILY QUESTIONS TO ASK EACH OF THE DREAMS YOU HAVE:

#1.) WHAT'S MY EXPERIENCE WITH THIS DREAM FROM LAST NIGHT?

#2.) HOW DOES THIS DREAM IMPROVE THE FORCE I'M WORKING ON?

DAY #3—WEDNESDAY—THE MOVING FORCE

As I trust you'll soon see, the number of dreams you dream may vary every night. One night you'll have three or four dreams; the next night you'll have a short one. That's what I had last night, and yet-- as I hope you will learn—short ones can have a lot of dream power.

And don't ever think that the few words of a dream are not worth your while to work on. Often, you will find that few words have great meaning and help you start to improve the Force that you're working on.

Keep in mind as you make your Forces thrive, how your goals thrive.

Now here's that very short dream that I wrote down—not too long after I went to sleep:

    *   *   *   *

Dream #1: 'It was quite odd killing people...And I see a bare-clothed leg that's standing upon the chest of some supine fellow who cannot move. (It's a symbol of conquering.)'

Now remember: my first task is to recall this dream and experience the scene. It only took a minute or two for me to do that: There was a hairy leg of a guy fixed upon the chest of another fellow whom I took to be dead. That hairy leg made me think the guy was some kind of a barbaric warrior. I guessed that the guy he's standing on may have been clothed in a formal style-- showing a civilized past.

The dream startled me as it showed one man having conquered and killed another man. That's all I saw.

Now how could this dream help to improve my Moving Force? Already, in the dream, I had said, 'How odd it was killing people!' Had I ever thought that in my real life? Had I ever thought how odd that--all over the world-- people kill people daily.

I don't know that I had ever called it 'odd'. I'm sure I've shuddered at the terror that war creates for folks— how it breeds killers out of regular everyday folks. But I never thought, 'How

ODD all that killing is!' So now how does such a thought help to improve my Moving Force? I think it makes me more aware of how mad it is that men are driven to stand upon the chests of unknown vanquished fellow beings.

I don't know that I can do anything more than to process the horror this is. Yet, doesn't that make me more inclined to never relish war or to look upon war as much more evil than just mankind acting so strange and odd to fellow men? Wouldn't that thought maybe change my behavior towards others in some caring way?

You see, here is a dream that comes from within me—it's not coming from other folks… It's not something I read or saw in the movies. It's coming from me; and to my mind it's intended to help me start to live a more thriving life. It feeds me with a strong nourishing thought that can only help me become someone whose behavior Is starting to reflect a better influence than perhaps what it had before.

Yet, there is a risk that when you fill your mind with an image like the one shown here you may be more likely to take on a habit that is harmful to behavior.

Smoking is a moving sort of habit; and when you are having dreams like this one, you may be apt to guide your Moving Force to what is congruent with such vile dreams.

So: suppose when you have such a dream as this one, you take it to mean you're supposed to conquer weaker souls? This is where I'd suggest you steer clear of any meanings that will sway and lead you to a negative deed. I think a lot of times folks get messages from dreams and interpret them wrongly.

I look upon dreams as guidance that helps me to lead a more thriving way of life.

Any action that hurts others or leads me into ways, which are harmful for me, is no action to be part of. If you'll stick with a line of positive thinking, you will find your life improving.

YOUR GOALS: TO BE SMOKE-FREE AND STRIVE TO BE THRIVING

DAY#4—THURSDAY—THE FEELING FORCE

IMPROVE YOUR FEELING FORCE THROUGH DREAMS—TO ACHIEVE YOUR GOALS!

WRITTEN UP DREAMS	*JOTTED DOWN DREAMS*

DAILY QUESTIONS TO ASK EACH OF THE DREAMS YOU HAVE:

#1.) WHAT'S MY EXPERIENCE WITH THIS DREAM FROM LAST NIGHT?

#2.) HOW DOES THIS DREAM IMPROVE THE FORCE I'M WORKING ON?

DAY #4—THURSDAY—THE FEELING FORCE

You may have started to ask, "How do you know that the dreams you are dreaming have a thing to do with the Force that you are working on?...How are you sure that dreams follow the sort of ideas that you are exploring?... After all, none really knows how dreams operate or what their real purpose might be...."

What you ask shows intelligence!

You have probably learned by now that a lot of things in life don't' always make sense. It's like a magician who makes things appear out of thin air. You've learned that's a trick; and it's true that people have been trying to find out the meaning of dreams for years. Why should what I'm doing be any better than what someone else has attempted? Can I really prove that a dream that I had last night can truly have some meaning for helping me improve the Force I'm working on?

Yet, these questions might be close to: can anyone prove that the person he falls in love with is the right one for him? Might it not happen that along the way he has discovered the loved person is not all that was cracked up? It's a challenge that calls for giving it his best effort.

If what I am showing you bears some fruit in your life—it keeps you from smoking and helps you start to live a life that is more thriving-- then I suggest that you give this Ninth Graders' Dream Primer some credibility.

But if you get deeper into this book and merely find that what I am saying really doesn't work well for you, then, like the lad who has tried his best and found his loved one wanting, "Adios me."

...The older I get the more I find that there are literally thousands of things that some people believe in while others do not. The key step for you as a young person is to note if there's something here for you.

...Since this is now the fourth day of the week (Thursday) let me go over what I dreamed: I propose to learn if this dream has some validity for improving the Force I'm working on—(The Feeling Force).

*   *   *   *

Dream #1: 'There's a huge expensive luxury car that seems to represent great wealth. The folks who are involved with this car don't seem to be so attached to it. It's as if they're used to having money and luxurious things. (Is that the way I'd like to be?)'

Do you recall what you do first? You ask yourself, "What's the experience I had in the dream that I had last night?"

So that's what I do first. Well, this car looks like one of those Bentley's that sells for two hundred thousand dollars. Maybe you have seen one. This Bentley was polished bright green. Did I feel some envy—jealousy or sadness? Did my tongue hang out as it passed? Is having one of these a goal that I cherish? Maybe years past...but not so now.

Still... maybe I have not admitted to myself: 'a car is a car to drive in—not something to have so I can puff my chest out.'

I liked the thought that the folks in the dream were not attached to this car. If they could afford to buy it, that is fine — but they did not hold it towards their bosoms as if their hearts were glued to how it looked.

So here I was feeling that I would want to be like these folks —not attached to wealth. (Do you see what I'm taught?) Not to get caught up in wealth—if wealth should drop upon me. And if wealth doesn't come, that's not so bad either.

We all need to have some comforts—you've probably already learned of the basic ones-- food, clothing, and shelter ... but to get attached to more things, may not be the best thing.

...So having worked on this dream and the experience I have had with it, I may sort of take a deep breath... as if a truth has been shown me. And though I don't know it, I'm drawn closer to avoiding a habit like smoking and nearer a life that is like a plant starting to thrive.

This particular Force— the Feeling Force—is one which we often forget about. Of course, we all live with our feelings all day long… but perhaps we never really learn to express them by writing them down ourselves. It's tough for us boys more than for girls to start doing this. But all of us should start.

It's surprising how keen you'll feel when you hold your dreams and write experiences which you have when you ponder them.

Some of you may never have ever written stuff, and you may feel strange doing it. But you will start to thrive in a true comfort zone and delight in new awareness.

YOUR GOALS: TO BE SMOKE-FREE AND STRIVE TO BE THRIVING

DAY#5—FRIDAY—THE THINKING FORCE

IMPROVE YOUR THINKING FORCE THROUGH DREAMS—TO ACHIEVE YOUR GOALS!

WRITTEN UP DREAMS	*JOTTED DOWN DREAMS*

DAILY QUESTIONS TO ASK EACH OF THE DREAMS YOU HAVE:

#1.) WHAT'S MY EXPERIENCE WITH THIS DREAM FROM LAST NIGHT?

#2.) HOW DOES THIS DREAM IMPROVE THE FORCE I'M WORKING ON?

DAY #5—FRIDAY—THE THINKING FORCE

Here's one dream I wrote down during the course of this fifth night. Let's see what it tells us:

*   *   *   *

Dream #1: "You never take your game very seriously." A fellow is talking to a group of others. He shows them a huge circle—it may be three feet diameter. Then he talks a little about it. "Maybe", he says, "We're born with just a plain circle." Now he adds two braces to make it much sturdier. He says, "People should add these in." Then he says, "You never take your game seriously…as you ought to."

When I glanced at this dream—after I had awakened in the morning-- it occurred to me that the man speaking must be someone that I should seriously study; and that I ought to tell you all that this man told his group.

Wouldn't you say that you might resemble this man's group that he's lecturing to? Yet I suspect some of you could take umbrage at what he says. ..

I trust a fair number of you do take the game of life keenly; and I regret hurting any of you by closely quoting him. But for the sake of what we all are attempting to do: to request dreams for our guidance—trusting dreams for guidance—all of you might admit that heretofore you have not taken the game (of life) with as much concern as what we're here talking about.

I think this dream's a gift to us. First of all, just getting such a revelation is mind-boggling. It's as if the source from whence dreams issue is really trying to help us achieve the goals we have.

The task isn't simple, is it?—working with dreams to help improve our Thinking Force so that-- along with the other Six Forces—we can proceed to keep from smoking and—more--to start living a life that is thriving?

This dream improves my Thinking Force by encouraging me in provocative ways to hopefully get you to think.

How seriously have you thought of your young life?

…Also the dream's given us a theme to start working on. "What is the theme?" You ask. It concerns the circle that we possess when we are born. It's just a plain circle. Yet if we don't strengthen it some, then its weakness will tend to reveal that we have failed to take life seriously.

So how and why do we add two braces to our plain old circle? We do this by beginning to use dreams to improve our Forces so that we can achieve our goals— which (as you know) are: to keep from smoking and to start to live life to be thriving.

…I hope by this day you are starting to dream dreams. There's no set way to capture them, though, technologically ,I keep things quite simple: I use a clipboard with paper clipped under the top part. I have a small flash light and a ball point pen tabled near. When I have a dream and wake up soon after, I engage my pen and the light and copy down the dream to the best of my recall. I write all the words that come to mind-- as I recall the dream-- and never block out any words from being written.

If I don't wake from a dream until morning time, I ask myself: 'What did I dream?' And immediately I write what I recall. There's a word "PAUSE"— which I try to remember to say, which strangely can bring back a dream I had, which I'd forgotten. I'm not sure how that works, but I urge you to try using it when you wake up—and see for yourself if it doesn't retrieve a dream.

Once you've recalled a dream or two-- always try to express your gratitude for what you've written down. You are dealing with an amazing part of your Unconscious; and letting it know how glad you are in receiving something from it—I have surmised-- encourages it to help more.

YOUR GOALS: TO BE SMOKE-FREE AND STRIVE TO BE THRIVING

DAY#6—SATURDAY—THE HIGHER FEELING FORCE

IMPROVE YOUR HIGHER FEELING FORCE THROUGH DREAMS—TO ACHIEVE YOUR GOALS!

WRITTEN UP DREAMS	*JOTTED DOWN DREAMS*

DAILY QUESTIONS TO ASK EACH OF THE DREAMS YOU HAVE:

#1.) WHAT'S MY EXPERIENCE WITH THIS DREAM FROM LAST NIGHT?

#2.) HOW DOES THIS DREAM IMPROVE THE FORCE I'M WORKING ON?

DAY SIX—SATURDAY—THE HIGHER FEELING FORCE

As may sometimes happen, something inside of us forbids us from recalling dreams. I'm positive we have them—maybe countless dreams each night-- but we don't recall them. Why? It is hard to say. Deep down, I think it is because we are not ready to deal with what they tell us. Sometimes, maybe, because we have not dealt with prior dreams— which were gifts to us--but that we chose to ignore.

For me--last night-- I'm fairly sure: I experienced dreams swirling around in me— but I couldn't muster the will to zero in on them.

Today with the Higher Feeling Force to work on, maybe that wasn't the right Force to use dreams to improve. ... Or maybe I wasn't' ready.

Certainly both this Force and the Higher Thinking Force surely stand above the rest. The other Five Forces live in our lives always— whereas these top Two Forces don't.

If you were to ask me what do these Two Forces do, my guess is they are Forces that have to do with the arts like architecture, music and song as well as those holy horizons and grand inventions of men... anything that springs from a source which is way out of our normal life circumstance.

But I opine that all of us have these Higher Forces snoozing away in us. Perhaps, if we revere them and seek specific guidance through our dreams, we may gain the benefit of their genius.

So many people have been turned on to something that pushes them to produce things that aggrandize greatly for their own welfare as well as for the world's welfare. What stems from lonely minds stretches across the world.

We shortchange our leonine lives if we think only men and women other than ourselves can come up with great things. One of the purposes of this book is to help introduce you:

that all you need to transform parts of your life are new insights and fresh perspectives you get from dreams.

One cardinal way to apply them is to have specific goals and your Seven Forces focused in mind. That said: when you dream dreams, you need a plan to direct them towards those Seven Forces and those specific goals.

It makes sense that by directing your goals here: to keep from smoking and to live a thriving life, you are dispatching your attention to what is quite worthwhile for you.

Many folks who smoke seem quite smart and--in many cases-- successful in their lives. And yet--with their habit—they can't help but forfeit the chance to live a thriving life. Their habit has to deflect all of their Seven Forces to a negative realm. Folks can't suck in cigarette smoke and not harm their lungs, their heart and numerous cells. They cannot smoke and not harm their Sexual Force and their Moving Force. And they can't inhale fumes and not misdirect their Feeling Force and their Thinking Force. Those Forces cannot function in proper health-- once they've been smitten with the scourge of tobacco.

Good men and fine women can be great even if they smoke—but they can never be thriving people—they can never be wholesome folk with their Forces in harmony.

We can't see what goes on behind the veiled surface of folks. If we could see what's going on, we would be appalled with the awful harm therein.

Folks can impress us outwardly: with how they dress, speak and dazzle us with talent, but they cannot hide from the fact that within them smoking's doing terrible things.

…Hopefully, none of you will dare take up this habit, lest you experience the dread truth of what smokers endure.

YOUR GOALS: TO BE SMOKE-FREE AND STRIVE TO BE THRIVING

DAY#7—SUNDAY—THE HIGHER THINKING FORCE

IMPROVE YOUR HIGHER THINKING FORCE THROUGH DREAMS—TO ACHIEVE YOUR GOALS!

WRITTEN UP DREAMS	*JOTTED DOWN DREAMS*

DAILY QUESTIONS TO ASK EACH OF THE DREAMS YOU HAVE:

#1.) WHAT'S MY EXPERIENCE WITH THIS DREAM FROM LAST NIGHT?

#2.) HOW DOES THIS DREAM IMPROVE THE FORCE I'M WORKING ON?

DAY SEVEN—SUNDAY—THE HIGHER THINKING FORCE

From Day Six with no dreams to this past night when I found myself with at least three dreams…This is the sort of thing that can happen to you. You'll wonder what you ought to do. It's not like your whole day can be spent on your dreams. You'll almost wish you were dream-free. And yet maybe you'll find startling gems in those dreams. It's a toss-up between being grateful for so many and wishing you had less.

Regardless of how many dreams… keep an even keel and be grateful to the source. Balance your dreams against your life. You simply may not have enough time in the day to examine so many dreams. I understand; I've been there hundreds of like times. Do the best with the "tools" you have.

Remember, you are in the process of using your dreams to help improve the Force that you are working on. Your intention in all of this is to keep from smoking and strive to be thriving.

Just making an effort to achieve these goals is enough to coax you towards success. Often, in some weird way, we touch where we are trudging towards — even if we fear we are failing to follow all the guideposts in a night's dreams.

If you simply commence to remember your dreams and follow through-- writing dreams down and devoting detailed time looking them over-- you will have made a splendid start.

Gradually, you can begin to see how your dreams might improve the Force you're on. As you start improving there, you should begin to sense in yourself more self-esteem and a sense that you are beyond smoking and close to living a life that's thriving.

For now, let me try to show you how I approached the three dreams I dreamed this past night:

*   *   *   *

Dream #1: 'I was talking with a guy about producing a movie. I naturally had to admit I'm no film producer and know little about doing it. But I thought that he might be interested. It starts out with a boat coming to shore--Then a meeting of a couple of men. Then I recall just this: we were standing and talking in a large hall with a backdrop of some large picture—filled with grey hues.'

Now let me tell you what I think I have learned from working with dreams for fifty years: there's the part of us that could look at this dream and drone to ourselves, "I haven't a clue as to what this dream means." That part's our "dumb self". Then there's the part that "opens up"-- when we sit down and take pen and paper or a blank computer sheet and write down or type out words that come through our hearts without thought. It's possible it's part nonsense, but often what we come up with is quite worthwhile.

I think folks who publish stories--call them professionals— sense this inner talent and use it each time that they write. And you'll emulate how they do it-- by simply attempting it.

Don't be fearful. What you are striving for is a unique effort; and once you make it, you may be heartened from what you have been able to learn: from attempting to experience the dreams that you have dreamed.

…So let's see what I've done with this first dream that I've shown you:

First I ask myself, 'What's my experience with this first dream that I dreamed last night?'

I love movies. Often I have published movie reviews and blogs for a few friends. It would be exciting to have an idea from which a film could be produced. But I don't fool myself. Film writing is a tough endeavor; and most of the time it takes writers years to get something good produced. But perhaps I could interest a producer in some idea that I have— an idea that seems worthwhile-- so he could then go and produce the film himself.

…I scarcely know a producer to approach, but it is possible that I might someday meet one and pitch to him

But how does this dream help to improve my Higher Thinking Force? It grants that Force a creative dimension it never had before. Whether something happens or not… having this sort of dream lights a fire within that's robust if chance favors it. Such an expectation provides our inner life with a glow that permeates all.

But here's another thought that has just come to mind. Maybe you are the "producers". You produce dreams that are pretty close to movies. I'm giving you new ideas as to how you can come up with your own movies. I can't tell you what you should do, but I can help show you how you go about it — with ideas I share with you.

Using this dream to help me apprehend that I can do something that will help you also strengthens this Force: its strength grows with service.

Now, had you asked me--before I wrote all of this—"What's my experience here?"—I would have become tongue-tied and shrugged off any chance that I could convey these new thoughts.

Now let me take you to Dream #2:

   *   *   *   *

Dream #2: 'Seated across from each other at a rather large table, I was explaining to a guy how to play a ball game by hitting the ball quite hard against the top of the table, so the ball doesn't go past his opponent—but keeps its presumed trajectory very high so he can stop it; and then he'll pound it not quite straight downwards, so it projects back to the partner. There was a garment on the table top that interferes with playing now, but I could at least tell how the game works.

Here, again, I would be without words to faintly say what my experience is with this above-mentioned dream tale. But applying myself to experiencing what it might be--by typing it—I will attempt to nail down just what I now sense:

On the face of it, the game seems terribly silly and pointless beyond ping pong. In ping pong you hold small paddles, have a rational goal in your outlook as you hit a small white ball, and make sure you serve it within lines on the opponent's side of the table.

With what I've dreamed, you pound a larger ball (maybe tennis ball-size) onto the top of the table and hope when it comes up it goes to the other side where someone there receives it and quickly hits it back. It seems an irksome sport— although in the dream I didn't consider it irksome.

Now the fact that there is a garment on the table—which keeps play from happening-- seems idiotic, too. Couldn't someone remove the wrap?

As I think about how one would have to hit the ball, it almost looks as if he would have to hit it sort of back and along his side-- so that the ball would go in the right trajectory to the opponent's side.

How does this dream improve the Force I am now working on? (Where is the point in this game?). Is it perhaps true that this game—which I'm attempting to explain-- is a bit like me explaining how to dream dreams? Am I making the game of dream work difficult to the point where you won't play it? Or is there more meaning that comes out of this dream?

Dreaming is not simple to share. It is like this game in that you almost have to hit the ball in a way that is far different from the way you would hit it in normal games of table tennis. And instead of playing against an opponent in ping pong —in this game I've dreamed-- which is quite difficult to get a handle on-- you hardly play the game in pairs.

When I explain how you hit the ball, it is sort of like what you do with this work: you aim sort of backwards, because you are saying to yourself: 'My forward dreaming will only come when I prepare myself by my serving the thoughts of my goal back in time from the actual dream.' I say to myself—encouraging some inner part-- 'I'm going to improve the Force I'm working on' with any dreams I will soon have.

And then once you have the dream (dreams) you serve it (them) back to yourself to examine. I know this is a bit difficult to digest, but hopefully you'll see that there's some sense to what's expressed.

The garment on the top of the table keeps this game from happening as long as it is never removed. The garment stands for the "habit"(?) of not wanting to play this game that I've explained. "Habit" may seem like a bit much for us to mine meaning from--but as you proceed you will find key words convey a double sense you'll pick up. A garment once had the meaning of a habit—that is something worn over clothes. From that use developed the following meaning: "habit"-- as behavior that one has taken on without maybe wanting to assume it. That one word helps us to experience this dream.

If you now rise to say: "Hey! You can't believe we'd figure this out the way you do! You've been doing dreams for fifty years…We are only doing dreams a few days!"

Of course, you're right…Please understand: I would never expect you to do what I do, but I believe that on your own terms you will be able to pattern what you do after the way I'm doing it. Your dreams will be very different from mine… You will bring to your dreams your own life and the concerns that you have as a young person. But the crucial thing is that you will be able to learn from your dreams as I learn from mine.

…Really, you may get a lot more pertinent information from your dreams than I will get here from mine. I am not in ninth grade, and I'm in scant danger of starting to smoke.

The reason I am going through the process of what you'll do is to give you an example of how to do this thing. So don't ever despair when you think I do dreams better.

Don't let happen to you what once happened to me, when I went out on a golf course with a professional golfer. When I saw how well he played--next to my playing-- I practically gave up the sport. That was wrong. I should have just accepted that he was a pro; and all I wanted to do was play a little golf socially. Okay?

Here is the third dream that I dreamed last night:

    *   *   *   *

Dream #3: 'I see a man pull out with a load of steel. It's late for him delivering. I notice as he turns right at the main street —a car blocks him turning completely. Later I ask if that was rehearsed –for some point-- with the car that blocked him. He turns and addresses my name with "Mister" before it—asking me where I receive my newspaper. We enter the shop and he shows me an article about a shop that does ornamental iron work --having some sort of problem with a building firm.'

I ask myself the same question: what's my experience with this third dream last night? Now you need to know that the guy who drove the truck (who was named in the dream) turned out to be a masked two-faced phony. He worked for me a long time; and I sure longed to get rid of him numerous times, but circumstances would never let me do it. It strikes me he is trying to act like he's working hard, when he's just pretending. He even has a guy block him from continuing on. And when I question him, he won't answer but diverts my attention to something he thinks I need to know that's just in the day's newspaper.

Now how does this dream help to improve the Force I'm now working on?

In spite of my wanting to fire him— I never quite saw through the way he would manipulate. And though a long time has passed since I have seen him, any time we gain awareness, we strengthen our Forces.

But there's more for you here… A very smart thing a person can learn to do in life is spot a real phony. Someone has called this: the process whereby something in us buzzes and barks, "Bull shit!"-- when confronted with folks who lie. Yet before we become experts in spotting frauds, we need to be willing to spot our own tendencies here.

Dreams will help us fess up when we're living out our own days on some stage of a play that is quite dishonest. It may hurt us when we dream it— but our discomfort is a fair indicator that the dream is right on with the message it's bringing us.

Once you're mindful yourself: Be mindful of how others lie— when you hear the bull shit buzzer sound in your ear. Life becomes much more thriving, too.

YOUR GOALS: TO BE SMOKE-FREE AND STRIVE TO BE THRIVING

DAY#8—MONDAY—THE INSTINCTIVE FORCE

IMPROVE YOUR INSTINCTIVE FORCE THROUGH DREAMS—TO ACHIEVE YOUR GOALS!

WRITTEN UP DREAMS	*JOTTED DOWN DREAMS*

DAILY QUESTIONS TO ASK EACH OF THE DREAMS YOU HAVE:

#1.) WHAT'S MY EXPERIENCE WITH THIS DREAM FROM LAST NIGHT?

#2.) HOW DOES THIS DREAM IMPROVE THE FORCE I'M WORKING ON?

DAY EIGHT—MONDAY—THE INSTINCTIVE FORCE

"I did stupid" last night, which I want to warn you against doing. It's a killer as far as rewarding yourself with the fruits of unfeigned dream work.

Here's what happened: Sometime at night I dreamed a dream--hard to follow... filled with many blurred images. I could only recall bits and pieces of it; but before I started to write down the parts I recalled, something within me chose not to write down a word...

I made the mistake of judging beforehand the parts I could put in words; and the more I prejudged their worth, the less I wanted to write them.

Whines went through my body, saying: 'They make no sense to me.'... 'Why should I deal with them?'... 'I'm simply not up to the task'...'How in the world do I know where I should begin?'... 'I haven't the slightest inkling about what I'm getting—if I write this stuff down...'

With every whine, I kept waiting. As the night wore on—and I kept coming back to my decision to write nothing-- the memory of the single parts of the dream became less and less clear to me. And it is now-- as I talk about what happened—that I have no idea of anything that they said.

You see: had I just gone ahead and put down on paper anything I recalled, I would now have something to talk about and attempt to experience. Perhaps, they'd all have been nonsense; but probably there would have been a spark or two of sense that might have held meaning.

Judging the worth of any dream --with your conscious mind—as you come to from sleep--is not using your judgment well.

I cannot tell you how often a dream that I would have taken to be worth naught turns out to be something that's worth a lot to me.

So how could I— with all the time I have spent working with dreams—been so mistaken to neglect to write these dream-parts? Unfortunately, I can be as lazy as the next guy if I permit it.

As you're reading this, you may find yourself thinking: "I haven't yet had any dream-- nor do I feel fit yet to start recalling one— so all your talk about leaving a dream, unwritten, strikes me as far ahead of where I am now."

I follow you; and that reminds me to say: as a child learns to walk after he has made effort upon effort, you, too, will become more aware of having dreams; and when you do, never ever decide to neglect its small parts.

Let me give you an example— also gleaned from a whole dream that I wrote last night: All I recalled was "U HUMITZ". Remember this was the dream-part; and it's up to me to give it a chance to be experienced by me..

Well, it just so happens that I try to practice a plain form of meditation—it's really just sitting… and a thing that I learned to do many years ago—from a dream that I had then— was to hum with lips closed tightly. I was never sure if I should do this humming the full thirty minutes I sat or just off and on as 'now hum' occurred to me.

Now let's step back to the first step: what's my experience with this dream-part last night? As I tried to experience this irrational phrase made of seven letters— it dawned on me, it's telling me: "You (will) hum it (to) Z." In other words, "Hum for the full length of the time (to Z)." I might add that this phrase was written on a wall— as if to make things crystal clear that I should not-- for a moment—overlook it.

…So that was my experience…Now you may ask, "So how does that phrase help improve my Instinctive Force?" I don't know for sure, but I suspect that humming--while I sit—builds up some kind of subtle strength-- connected with the throat and lungs and the larynx. There is also a sensation that one gets humming, which is sort of a tickle that touches the tip of the lips, which is stimulating.

I have no definite knowledge of what health this might bring, but I'll hazard a guess it could benefit the stability of the Instinct.

YOUR GOALS: TO BE SMOKE-FREE AND STRIVE TO BE THRIVING

DAY#9—TUESDAY—THE SEXUAL FORCE

IMPROVE YOUR SEXUAL FORCE THROUGH DREAMS—TO ACHIEVE YOUR GOALS!

WRITTEN UP DREAMS	*JOTTED DOWN DREAMS*

DAILY QUESTIONS TO ASK EACH OF THE DREAMS YOU HAVE:

#1.) WHAT'S MY EXPERIENCE WITH THIS DREAM FROM LAST NIGHT?

#2.) HOW DOES THIS DREAM IMPROVE THE FORCE I'M WORKING ON?

DAY NINE—TUESDAY—THE SEXUAL FORCE

One risk I wanted to caution you about is the way life cuts into your dream work: you may rue a night or two of missing dreams... Events may cause distraction in your home life that prevents you from focusing on any dreams that you have at night; and at times you may just subconsciously need a rest from nightly monitoring of the dreams you may have. Do not be disheartened.

Once I had to go out of town for a week, where I could not capture any dreams. When I returned, I simply picked up from where I left off; and no great loss occurred to the dream work I was doing.

...My wife and I heard of a dear friend who was in the hospital with a sudden emergency, which called for an operation; but when doctors got to the place that needed fixing, it was beyond their repair. We tried to keep abreast of what was happening, but all we could do was wait by the phone and speak with other friends.

I mention this as the sort of crisis that comes into all our lives; and against such disconcerting dread, dream work gets demoted to a lesser force in our lives.

But even at times like that, it is possible to see if you can relax and sow a few moments, so you can review the dreams that you've had in the past few days.

It's dismaying how fast dreams become diminished-- that we've only recently dreamed. Reinforcing their thrust by repeating them out loud is something I try to do.

One service I wanted to provide you with at this time was a disclosure of what I repeat during bedtime. Whether it helps me--without doubt-- to recall dreams-- I cannot guarantee —but I feel as if it might just make an impression on the Unconscious—as a sincere signal to it I really want to recall dreams:

"Oh Inner Being who rules my every moment: encour-

age my mind and body to remember my dreams and put them into words so that I can study them well. I promise I will not take this gift for granted but will cherish it every day."

I also say the next two inner directives:

"Oh Moving Force who is the one who writes down dreams: I pray that you'll cooperate and write down everything that I happen to dream without any hesitancy."

And:

"I pray that I may be quick to say 'PAUSE' just when I awaken—so to recall any dreams or remnants of dreams that I may have and then promptly to write them down."

As I said, I believe that these three directives aid areas of dream resource to be amenable to my dreaming dreams and retaining them without delay.

You may want to create your own dream directives, which suit you more agreeably.

At the other end of the dream spectrum—results-- I should like to share with you five enlightened sayings I've received directly from dreams. Each word is as I dreamed it. They may impress you with their wise lucidity, which your own dreams might give you, too:

(1.) We have to love things as we also find ourselves reacting against them.

(2.) Love is the universal elixir.

(3.) We would love to be able to jump on stuff and process it immediately.

(4.) Feel good, think good, do well—that should be uppermost in one's mind.

(5.) Fill your mind and heart with love.

I should add that these five sayings are just a few of the countless ones that I've dreamed over the past years. I cherish all sayings from my dreams as gifts. I don't feel they're for preaching to others; yet I wanted to give you what I call proof of how dreams can help you be attuned towards thriving in your life.

Dreams can also be specific about thoughts you might want to implement: hobbies, new interests, or decisions.

YOUR GOALS: TO BE SMOKE-FREE AND STRIVE TO BE THRIVING

DAY#10—WEDNESDAY—THE MOVING FORCE

IMPROVE YOUR MOVING FORCE THROUGH DREAMS—TO ACHIEVE YOUR GOALS!

WRITTEN UP DREAMS	*JOTTED DOWN DREAMS*

DAILY QUESTIONS TO ASK EACH OF THE DREAMS YOU HAVE:

#1.) WHAT'S MY EXPERIENCE WITH THIS DREAM FROM LAST NIGHT?

#2.) HOW DOES THIS DREAM IMPROVE THE FORCE I'M WORKING ON?

DAY TEN—WEDNESDAY—THE MOVING FORCE

It requires steadfast degrees of discipline to always ask this question first: "what's my experience with this new dream last night?" That is what we should always ask. So right after we've read this first dream, let's ask it.

     *   *   *   *

Dream #1: 'Someone got involved with an old builder on a house: Somehow if something doesn't happen with this cheap house deal, Buyer must pay so much per month (say two hundred a month times twelve months equals two thousand four hundred times five hundred years...) When I call my doctor about some matter, he, too, is quite concerned about what happens to him if his patient (Buyer) doesn't understand this deal. I was puzzled because I couldn't recall my knowing anything or having any folder with this information in it. I had the raw feeling I had somehow overlooked it.'

What's my experience with this first dream last night?

Let's not strive to make sense at first. Let's work with what our own experience is now. Yes, it's a dream that makes no sense of what the deal's about: Buyer must either see through what she is getting involved with—or buy a cheap house— and pay one million bucks in the course of five hundred years.

Who's so villainous to dare offer such a choice? The builder's name, unhappily, sounds close to: FAT OR ROT. (We'll deal with that shortly.) There's also a doctor involved, who's quite worried about his own reputation-- if his patient accepts the deal. There we have: pretty much the dream experience.

Now let's ask how the dream might help improve our Moving Force.

Moving is "behavior". When we hear of behavior in folks' lives —behavior the same for years—say, the way youths keep smoking right through dotage-- we must guess such folks have shrugged off calamities they'll surely find "way down the road".

Maybe they grab up those cigarettes (as a cheap house) costing less then they would think— without recognizing that they've been sucked into a harsh "mortgage" that goes on for nearly eternity-- (five hundred years to youths)

It's simple to assert: buyers-cum-smokers act just as naïve as anyone. Why would these would-be-smokers stoop to choose a "cheap house" (called cigarettes) and then go along blindly with a "mortgage" that takes them well past death?

Let's look at the builder— whose last name sounds like FAT-OR-ROT...FAT OR ROT seems the choice given by the builder. He must think girls—more so than boys-- --are forced to choose between smoking and being fat. (Ads do feature slim girls smoking.) Do girls prefer ROTTING (from illness in old age) to being fat while in their prime? Just like the buyer who gets a house cheap but then is plagued with an evil mortgage: would these young girls rather start out cheap with smoking now and deal with rotting later? The truth is smoking does not guarantee slimness. (A thriving life might well do that.)

So how does this dream help improve the Moving Force we're working on?

It grants insight in a way we've not seen. It warns against smoking as it shows us what an awful bargain we get into: by agreeing to smoke (like purchasing a house cheaply) --never realizing the long term debt we'll pay.

Thank goodness for the gift of dreams!

...Onward to the second dream that I dreamed last night:

*   *   *   *

Dream #2: 'A friend of ours becomes a meditation guide. For some reason all seven of our friends go in for a session... but I'm delayed. Before, I found bananas for our group and throw one of them against a wall. A visitor turned to me and said, "You are tough!" One of the pieces of fruit was in a circle, and I handed it to one friend—insisting it was a banana as well. I had to barge into the meditation bout and found all the people on the floor with blankets that were covering their bodies. I said, 'They all look dead—God forbid!' With that they stirred a bit.'

What's my experience with last night's second dream?

It's easy to become baffled. I again urge you not to try to apprehend what a dream might mean, because your search could get stymied at the very beginning.

So let's stick with "experience".

I don't like to see folks being blindly led towards a discipline that's vague to them. I'm also suspicious of group get-togethers where people get the same answer from one person's query. We are all different.

When I saw all my friends huddled under their blankets-- as if they were fresh corpses-- I panicked and cried out dismayed. My loud agitation may have shocked them to life.

My throwing stuff against the wall showed me in defiance of the reality I felt my friends might be losing. Falsehood's what I could spot quicker here than they could.

So how's this dream improve the Force I am now working on? (Recall: the Moving Force.)

It's advising me not to act like the meditation guru who sought seven unsuspecting pupils to go along with his newfound life and then got "blanket" approval.

I want each of you to be your guru with your own set of standards.

Yes… I want you to come out of this program being keen to keep from smoking, and wanting to live to be thriving. But I do not lay down any dogmatic rules. Each of you should find your paths from your own revelations, which you'll get from your dreams.

This dream provides an example of what not to do as well as what should be done.. It's important that we learn that. There's nothing so worthwhile as getting the guideposts you'll need to live to be thriving.

YOUR GOALS: TO BE SMOKE-FREE AND STRIVE TO BE THRIVING

DAY#11—THURSDAY—THE FEELING FORCE

IMPROVE YOUR FEELING FORCE THROUGH DREAMS—TO ACHIEVE YOUR GOALS!

WRITTEN UP DREAMS	*JOTTED DOWN DREAMS*

DAILY QUESTIONS TO ASK EACH OF THE DREAMS YOU HAVE:

#1.) WHAT'S MY EXPERIENCE WITH THIS DREAM FROM LAST NIGHT?

#2.) HOW DOES THIS DREAM IMPROVE THE FORCE I'M WORKING ON?

DAY ELEVEN—THURSDAY—THE FEELING FORCE

I will attest to this: almost every dream is a challenge to your own will to experience and learn how that dream improves the Force that you are working on.

Much unexpected good comes from efforts you make. I have a sense that doing this work engages many unused talents we have. We call to parts of our being that have long lain dormant — and they wake up a bit.

Let's review the first dream last night:

* * * *

Dream #1: 'A friend of mine got the idea of building large clusters of residences in an area that's across the street from large condos. I had thought it was a way of giving back to the city for what he had already made in the way of profits. When I shared with him this thought I had, he denied it was non-profit. He was sort of stretched out on the ground as I stood above him with someone else.'

What's my experience with this first dream last night?

This friend of mine was an old friend, who unfortunately-- all his life—had never scored in any endeavors that he'd attempted; and he'd had plenty of cash from his father to give him the chance. Over time I'd sensed that he was competing with his dad—really a giant of a man in what he'd done. The harder his son tried to outmatch Dad, the more he failed.

Yet the son had a big heart; and there'd been friendship between us from the time we had been the youngest of kids. I must have remembered much of this past-- as he told me about his current plans. I think I sensed that he would not succeed in this, as well. I mean, there he was stretched out on the grass—instead of standing up on plucky feet.

So how does this dream help me improve the Feeling Force that I was now working on? Dreams can have value for more than the one dreamer. This one may have value for you.

Things don't occur because one happens to be rich or imagines bold ideas. One must commit oneself with more than his two lips to a passion that is within. Our feelings need to be educated with this sort of grounding— otherwise we'll amble along with a false expectation that our wiles and wealth will wring success… And if feelings stay faint, it becomes easy to take up smoking and never know what a life of thriving could fully amount to.

What might a dream to improve your Feelings look like? I have no way of predicting, but somewhere in you there's a dream that will come in your sleep and be of help to you.

Could it be that your Feeling Force is as well-formed as it should be-- without dream help? My idea of humankind is that every single one of us can stand growth— in the form of dreams-with-a-goal. If you dream without a goal—unlike what we've got— I think you'll lack the benefit of the energy that having goals produces. Yes, you might have one dream that helps, but I seriously doubt dreams cooperate over a long time period.

Here is the second dream that I recalled last night:
*   *   *   *

Dream #2: 'I was at a fairly large table that was filled with other folks—we're all involved in some accounting work. The sophisticated accounting talk went above my head, but in the meeting I seemed to be taken as a leader. Later on, a super accomplished guy (an acquaintance of mine) appears with his group and swiftly takes over the space that we'd been occupying; and when he did that, it simply left my own group searching for another large space that might now be available.'

What's my experience with last night's second dream?

Here was a group of accountants who professionally knew more about their field than I knew; and yet they'd allowed me to be their leader in some project that we all happened to be engaged in.

I am feeling in charge-- until suddenly an acquaintance of mine enters the room unannounced and with brusk braggadocio. He doesn't say anything like "Excuse us, or I hope you don't mind…or we have the permission to meet in here…" My feelings are bruised a bit, but I shrug it off and hope we'll find another space. Now, how does this dream help improve the Force I am now working on? (The Feeling Force)

We have to learn to shield our feelings against harm-- with a seasoned sense of humor. We really cannot be the guardians for how others treat us. They are their own..

Can our feelings be schooled? It's very important they are schooled—if we want to live a life that is thriving. We can't be ridiculed by someone's lack of good manners --regardless of who they are or what they have done. Their success may never come close to a life that's thriving.

Once we're able to craft our feelings so we don't cave in—when stuff like this happens--it's unlikely that we'll fall into the smoking habit. You may or may not know this: Smoking has a way of assuaging youths' hurt feelings. You don't ever want to be in a position where cigarettes become your crutch.

Here's another dream that I dreamed during this night:
*   *   *   *

Dream #3: 'A friend is visiting me, and I suggest we each have a smoke on our pipes. But then I ask my wife, 'Do you permit smoking in our living room?' She says, "No!" Then we start talking about an air purifier that other folks have that we could put in our house. I see—as she walks around—that a body of smoke engulfs her.

What's my experience with this third dream last night?

Now here's something that's pretty weird: I stopped smoking fifty- plus years ago—shortly after my wife and I married. Not once have I had a cigarette or pipe-full of tobacco. So having this dream is a strange surprise. It glosses over my act of smoking and focuses on my wife forbidding my living room smoking. It talks about purifiers as if that helps us stop. And it's puzzling that my wife's engulfed with a lot of smoke.

Also puzzling is that in the dream I never once recalled that I hadn't smoked for over fifty years. It was absolutely as if I were not the same guy.

How does this dream improve the Force I'm working on? (Remember: it's the Feeling Force.) One thing that we learn here: is that we often do things in our lives that are almost as if we're different. Let me give you a clear example: A man sees a friend die from smoking. He swears off the habit with all the force he has. A week later he's watching a football game that's a nail-biter…with seconds of time remaining and the score all tied up…Now his team gets the ball. In that instant-- his heart beating much faster than normal— he jumps up and grabs a cigarette pack out of a drawer (where there's one pack he had not thrown away last week) Quick as a wink, he lights one stick.

Is he the same person who swore off cigarettes seven days past? He's different. What's happened is one of his Forces (the Feeling Force) backed off its obligation or forgot what it pledged and took up the habit again.

Now here is the sad scoop: Having started smoking – with just one cigarette— (It's been proven time and a-gain.)-- there is very little that he can do to halt his new course of weakened action. He is once again hooked on this evil habit… He'll curse himself— and swear sadly — but once an ex-smoker picks up one cigarette, you can bet he's back to smoking.

Do you see why it's such an evil habit? It has no mercy to let one stop. How much simpler is it to never start at first!

Now back to the dream we're viewing. How does it help improve the Force I'm working on?

Could it be that this dream allows me to tell all of you what I have just told you— that regardless who we might be, we can still start smoking --if we are not careful. If a guy who's not smoked for more than fifty years—if he can start back with a pipe-- then anyone can start back, too. In other words, you, who have never yet smoked, should never think that it's a sure thing to stop-- once you've started. Forging feelings stronger with such advice helps life to thrive.

YOUR GOALS: TO BE SMOKE-FREE AND STRIVE TO BE THRIVING

DAY#12—FRIDAY—THE THINKING FORCE

IMPROVE YOUR THINKING FORCE THROUGH DREAMS—TO ACHIEVE YOUR GOALS!

WRITTEN UP DREAMS	*JOTTED DOWN DREAMS*

DAILY QUESTIONS TO ASK EACH OF THE DREAMS YOU HAVE:

#1.) WHAT'S MY EXPERIENCE WITH THIS DREAM FROM LAST NIGHT?

#2.) HOW DOES THIS DREAM IMPROVE THE FORCE I'M WORKING ON?

DAY TWELVE—FRIDAY—THE THINKING FORCE

Sometimes dreams deliver something quite specific that you can wrap your arms around... Currently, we're working on our Thinking Force, and the following dream is surely specific about how I can improve that Force.

Yet, please take note that what's evinced in this dream doesn't have to be something other folks need follow. This is the truth to always keep in mind. What is right for me is not something that you need follow.

But hopefully when you see how dreams work for me, you will have faith they'll work for you-- giving you all versions of experiences that will address chunks of your life.

So keeping that in mind, let's look at what this dream has advised me to take note of:

•   *   *   *

Dream #1: 'I was talking about several topics that seemed to impress others in the manner they responded. I said, 'I'll tell you, there's one magazine that can really make you feel that you're well informed about many subjects; and that's The New Yorker.'

What's my experience with this new dream last night?

I've subscribed to The New Yorker for many years—although in the last six months, I decided I would give it up. It was probably a mistake to have done that; for this dream seems to assert that it's something I should read.

How does this dream improve the Force that I am working on?

Again, for me, it says that this magazine gives me a thinking experience that is stimulating.

...So here's a magazine that I should choose to keep reading. On the other hand, you may dream of something that would be good for you to act on.

I want to add, though, that whatever the dream wants: may not be what you can act on. It may call out a book that's unavailable at the moment, or one you can't afford to buy right now. Then just keep it in mind; and possibly the time will come when somehow you will be able to obtain it.

Above all, have faith in you dreams.

I once had a dream with a food product disclosed that I had not ever heard of. I went to look it up on the Internet and was totally gratified that such a product existed.

It is tough for some folks to believe that you can have such a dream "out of the blue". They will try to get you to confess that somehow you heard about it before the dream disclosed it to you.

I'm inclined to gamble a guess that in some way we may be privy to all sorts of unknown facts-- and that rather than try to disdain the idea that we can learn from our dreams, we should adopt the opportunity of obtaining from dreams observations helpful for growth.

All too often, we sense in ourselves we're single units on earth; when in truth we may all be tethered to each other and to all the knowledge and gnosis that's now or ever existed.

That doesn't mean that you'll learn all answers solely from dreams; but that as you frame your effort to live a life that is thriving (for you, yourself) dreams may arrive with rare enlightenment to boot.

So many great inventions have come to people who have spent long nights attempting to figure out questions they've faced— only to have a dream appear with the answer.

There is so much hype in these times about all the progress that's daily being made through science and technology and education and higher mathematics.

How is all of this happening? My hunch is—whether it is sensed or not—so much is brought to folks from dreams they have.

As ninth graders you can become part of this scene and contribute all that you're worth by developing dreams, avoiding smoking, and living a life that is thriving.

Dreams should never become someone's escape from life— but more as a venue towards life.

Whatever positive influences you have in your life—your kin folk, teachers, your religious leaders, heroes in history, your better friends, dreams can be one more avenue for your development as a human being whom the world needs.

The thrill about dreams, which it would make sense to see, is that—unlike outside forces-- dreams come to us from the depths of our own being. Perhaps they can be trusted more or at least equally to forces outside us.

They're your resource that's unexplored.

YOUR GOALS: TO BE SMOKE-FREE AND STRIVE TO BE THRIVING

DAY#13—SATURDAY—THE HIGHER FEELING FORCE

IMPROVE YOUR HIGHER FEELING FORCE THROUGH DREAMS—TO ACHIEVE YOUR GOALS!

WRITTEN UP DREAMS	*JOTTED DOWN DREAMS*

DAILY QUESTIONS TO ASK EACH OF THE DREAMS YOU HAVE:

#1.) WHAT'S MY EXPERIENCE WITH THIS DREAM FROM LAST NIGHT?

#2.) HOW DOES THIS DREAM IMPROVE THE FORCE I'M WORKING ON?

DAY THIRTEEN—SATURDAY—THE HIGHER FEELING FORCE

Now I wish to remark about an aspect of dreaming that may have dawned on you-- even without telling you, as I now propose.

There's no statement that's absolute; but this may be said: dreams are often quite boring.

Nevertheless, sometimes someone may drag you to the side, and gasp, "Guess what I dreamed last night?" That dream could well turn out to be fascinating. But more than often, what others dream can scarcely ever elicit interest in what their dreams show you.

But the point is: dreams are not meant to be an exciting, spell-binding spectacle. Their sole purpose—conceived as I'm showing you in this book— is to guide you—alone—in pathways that improve Forces.

Each one of those Forces— whether it's Instinctive, Sexual, or Moving… Feeling or Thinking, or Higher Feeling …Higher Thinking… Each one of them does contribute towards your character and your ableness to be.

In general, no one's received direct education to improve their Forces. In this book, I am showing you a way to achieve two goals through the use of dreams that improve your Seven Forces. My primary object is to direct you to those two goals: First-- to keep you from smoking, and second: to guide you to live a life that is thriving. I believe that by willingly working each night and day on one of your Forces you'll encourage your dreams to provide an experience that will help you achieve each of those goals.

Dreams have been a resource for so many cultures— over many thousands of years—to help folks succeed.

It's been documented that night temples were once constructed for the express purpose of encouraging folks to come there and seek dream guidance, which might help them receive relief from maladies that were not then curable with the knowledge and skill held by other professions.

Dreams then were sought as quick fixes. Perhaps dream advisors would be on hand —eager to assist folks to interpret the dreams they dreamed that night.

In another age and region on earth, some Indian tribes had a custom of sending their young men to live in the woods— without any food, clothing or shelter… an initiation for their coming into manhood. The test for these youths would consist in readying themselves for dreams that would guide them towards a way to survive as well as to prescribe the sort of work or profession they should pursue in life for their tribe's benefit

I've heard of at least one instance where a tribal chief had a dream--outlining a ceremony his tribe should take on as a new custom that would encourage a new belief or understanding, which would result in some benefit to the tribe.

Without seeking, dreams may send help.

In every age leaders often find in a dream unsought guidance that helps them deal with some crisis they face.

However dreams may work, they're a resource that should be used in a systematic way to help reach one's goals. The system I am proposing for use by ninth graders may well be suitable for anyone with any goals.

Most dreams that I have dreamed-- as you've witnessed so far-- probably do not resonate as exciting stories. Yet my reason for their inclusion is to show how they're important in the way they can be used to help improve the Force I'm working on. It's not so much the dream, itself-- as the way that dream can be used--that's fulfilling. And you will find that your dreams can have the same great benefit to you in your life.

The vindicating deed-- that gives dreams their value— is when you are able to start experiencing the truth contained in a dream. A smile will come over your lips; a recognizable joy to your spirit, and --like a gift from your Unconscious— your breath may exhale in a way that lets you know what you've expressed is right for you.

No plethora of talk can ever penetrate the layers of your being as can your experiencing and improving with dreams. Experience always trumps talk. And experience—then improvement—begins when you remember these two key steps: 1.) What's my experience with this dream from last night? 2.) How does this dream improve the Force I'm working on?

YOUR GOALS: TO BE SMOKE-FREE AND STRIVE TO BE THRIVING

DAY#14—SUNDAY—THE HIGHER THINKING FORCE

IMPROVE YOUR HIGHER THINKING FORCE THROUGH DREAMS—TO ACHIEVE YOUR GOALS!

WRITTEN UP DREAMS	*JOTTED DOWN DREAMS*

DAILY QUESTIONS TO ASK EACH OF THE DREAMS YOU HAVE:

#1.) WHAT'S MY EXPERIENCE WITH THIS DREAM FROM LAST NIGHT?

#2.) HOW DOES THIS DREAM IMPROVE THE FORCE I'M WORKING ON?

DAY FOURTEEN—SUNDAY—THE HIGHER THINKING FORCE

Here's a brief dream I wrote down from last night, which burdened me with feelings of constraint.

*   *   *   *

Dream #1: 'I'm in lockstep, as I get set to catch a ball or hit with a tennis racket.'

What's my experience with this first dream last night?

I did not quite comprehend what the word "lockstep" meant, though as I said above, I had a feeling I was constrained.

It turns out that lockstep describes a kind of march (as in prison) where prisoners are forced to follow the step formation of the prisoner in front of them; and that procedure has to be strictly adhered to all the way down to the last man.

It's supposed to drill folks in a way that keeps them bunched together, so they can't go their own way or engage in conversation with any of the men around them.

So although in the dream I was prepared to play several games, it was as if I would not be playing with a sense of freedom.

(I have gotten into the dream's meaning way before I really intended to. I hope you will excuse me here, but sometimes that happens when I am not sure of what a word means...and look it up.)

Now let's continue and ask ourselves—or I will: how does this dream improve the Force that I am working on? (The Higher Thinking Force)

Evidently, this Force has not been encouraged to grow with very much freedom. I've been prompted to play sports-games that outwardly I thought I always liked playing... Yet, I never got very good in any of them, and bowed out earlier than most of my friends.

Thus--from this dream-- it appears that I played games—like a prisoner in lockstep with his fellow cons. Frankly, I'm not surprised to encounter this truth. What the dream leads me to devise is a brand new approach: that in place of those sports there may well be interests that will mean a lot more to me—even at my age.

Do you see how a dream like this sets me free from what I may have gone along with and guides me to something better?

…Continuing… I'll share the next dream from last night:

•   *   *   *

Dream #2: 'I'm looking for a ride and stand by a bus stop, which was also where vehicles picked up folks. One's supposed to be by in minutes. But along came a bus, and I got on. The driver took my fare and announced he was going to stop and take a break and have a coffee and cigarette. I fret with this delay. While the bus was stopped, I listened to some guy talk to the driver about some kind of business problem he's confronting—and seeking his advice. I envy the young fellow his challenge—but wonder how the driver could help him. Soon people were getting back to their seats, and I try to figure from memory where my seat would fit best with theirs.

What's my experience with last night's second dream??

One motif that appears in dreams is that which features a come-what-may-style of life.

In movies, plays and books we tend to be shown lives that are more exciting than ours. Generally, artists in those forms of exposition scarcely ever show lives as they're really lived day-by-day. They take snatches from lives that contain conflict; and create drama that compels us to be fully engaged in participation.

Dreams' agendas are different. Unlike art forms, dreams are here to help us improve. Even though our dreams don't embrace that much drama… doesn't mean they're not worth noting. Dreams may be sly as they conceal truths we might pass over or never consider.

So here we have a dream that seems to be about as dull as any dream could be. But let's take heed. There may be a surprise that awaits us...So far I do not know if what I sense is even right.

But let us ask again, "What's our experience with this second dream from last night?" (We should answer this as candidly as we can.)

I look as if I'm spending time waiting for a bus ride or someone to pick me up—to take me... where I don't say.

Am I just killing time with no notion in mind? That doesn't sound like a life that's even close to thriving. It's as if I say: 'I don't know what to do...so I'll just let someone else tell me.'

Next, I get on the bus. How'd you like a driver to take your fare and then announce he is taking a break?

(I went to a barber whose wont was to say-- as my turn came to get a haircut-- "Excuse me a few minutes, but I haven't had lunch yet." I understoodd the guy's got to eat, but it kind of made me smile at his way of conducting a business.)

...So this driver now stops the bus. As he sits there drinking coffee and smoking, too, I overhear a passenger asking advice from this man, who owns no business. Wouldn't you ask advice from a guy who HAS a business?

But let's remember this: it is my dream, and what's in it is something I need to experience, myself. To criticize the young fellow who's asking for advice-- and the driver, giving it-- may reflect on me, somehow. Or it may also be something I should show you.

Do any of us ask advice from people who have no experience doing what we're asking their advice on? For instance, if you turn to someone-- while you read this book-- and ask that person, who's never thought about dreams: "What do you think of this?"- You're bound to hear humdrum advice. Or if in your schooling, you seek some sound guidance on some matter from someone who's never been in school much, you are going to hear advice, which may sound fanciful. So the dream I have here may be for all of us.

The last part of the dream I need to experience is-- when it's time to sit down: What's going through my mind with that? I don't want to sit too close to the passengers. I want to pick a seat that is as isolated as I can possibly find. Why do I want to act like that? Am I afraid to sit next to another soul? Wouldn't that mark an opportune time to share with someone some aspect of our lives? If I sit off to myself, what benefit do I get? The answer is "Nothing". Whereas if I sit near people, is it not possible I will learn something new or share with them what they don't know?

I once knew a fellow who struck up a friendly conversation with a plane-mate; and it developed that he became his partner and ended up earning millions.

The raw truth is we have no idea who is on that bus and who we'll sit near, and the exposure could reveal a new resource.

Do you see how a dream which looked totally worthless turns out to be a teaching dream that opens up new insights? You may retort, "Yeah, but how am I going to get that much stuff out of my dreams?"

All I can say is, 'You will get precisely what you are equipped to get; and the readier you become, the more insights you'll have.' And my hope is your insights will lead you to understand that nothing in your life can be gained if you start smoking; and many things in your life can be gained when dreams help you to live to be thriving.

YOUR GOALS: TO BE SMOKE-FREE AND STRIVE TO BE THRIVING

DAY#15—MONDAY—THE INSTINCTIVE FORCE

IMPROVE YOUR INSTINCTIVE FORCE THROUGH DREAMS—TO ACHIEVE YOUR GOALS!

WRITTEN UP DREAMS	JOTTED DOWN DREAMS

DAILY QUESTIONS TO ASK EACH OF THE DREAMS YOU HAVE:

#1.) WHAT'S MY EXPERIENCE WITH THIS DREAM FROM LAST NIGHT?

#2.) HOW DOES THIS DREAM IMPROVE THE FORCE I'M WORKING ON?

DAY FIFTEEN—MONDAY—THE INSTINCTIVE FORCE

Last night was a dry spell as far as capturing dreams that I had. I did dream dreams, but--like a hunter with a loaded gun who can't quite harvest birds that fly beyond-- I couldn't hold any dreams in mind long enough to put ballpoint pen to paper.

It is at times like these when the best I can do is to scramble and scrawl something-- even if it's a phrase or a couple of words. Yet doing that, I always dread the bits I've written will read like nonsense in the light of day when I review them.

But quite often, even small scraps of a dream will offer advice that is worthwhile.

When you start "doing dreams", I encourage you to always write down whatever's dreamed. You may sense it's nonsense, but at least your dream source will sense you've got spunk to keep at it.

...Now to the dream that's here: Let me review it and then see what sense it might have.

•   *   *   *

Dream #1: 'There was something about U-Z is a shelter. There's another symbol someone had told me was the same. (Unfortunately, the other part of the dream was lost.)'

Are we wasting time when we work on dreams like this? Or could value emerge from our simply plodding along? In other words—even though in our minds they make no sense—could it be that gain will come from our diligence?

How can we grow if we're wary to explore the obscure?

Hey, no one's keeping score; and just maybe we'll uncover guidance we've never got.

I say: we should attempt to gain guidance from this brief dream.

So we'll take the same step that we have been taking—
that is, asking the key question:

What's my experience with this first dream last night?

Well, I was keen to adopt the new symbol in "U-Z" to stand for a shelter— but I was stung that the other word for shelter vanished before I could hold it in my mind to quickly write it.

But one thing I have found-- when I have lost key contents of a dream I've had-- is that the loss might mean I'm not fit to keep it. It's like someone's holding up a prize in front of me and proclaiming, "Ah, but you are not ready to receive this! You need to work harder, be persistent, and then maybe someday you will get it!"

So even if we can't experience the dream, perhaps we are being taught to become persistent in life with other projects.

Do you follow what I'm saying?

You know: most people—when they seek after something -- get rebuffed by galling events, cold strangers or mishaps -- forcing them to give up.

But when you seek something strongly, you should never give up or let your passion die.

A fellow once called me on the phone (when I owned a steel company years ago); and here is how he addressed me: "Hey! You're not looking for a welder are you?" (How badly was he wanting a job?) It almost seemed as if he wanted me to say "No"—which I did. He then explained he needed folks' three "No's"-- at which point he'd phone the unemployment people and tell them he had tried to get a job and was turned down. His "efforts" would entitle him for unemployment bucks. (Calls in that vein are no way to get work.)

Perhaps this dream was directing me, so I'd benefit from it and share it with you; and we'd all learn that persistence is one of the shrewdest tools a person can have to succeed..

Now, startlingly, if I ask how this dream improves my Instinctive Force, it just might be that the "shelter" in the dream (U-Z) is what is needed to be persistent.

What then is that shelter? The shelter is what keeps us protected from giving up-- when we are likely to fail in early attempts. U-Z could stand for: "U" (you/ me) go the full way to "Z" (making countless attempts) By then we may get what we seek.

Now you may think I am going too far with that "symbol— U-Z", but perhaps it's a prop we can use when we're trying to succeed. We think, "U-Z!" when we call up people for summer jobs— or go by and pitch them. It reminds us that our shelter is our conviction that we will not be undone or broken when someone says, "No".

Kentucky Fried Chicken's founder—Colonel Sanders— heard nine hundred "No's" before he finally got someone to sell his fried chicken. How many "No's could we withstand?

...Here's the second dream from last night:

•   *   *   *

Dream #2: 'People are going to a kitchen when something happens.'

What's my experience from last night's second dream?

I imagined that the people going to the kitchen were most likely going there to eat or prepare food; and some were going there when mood swings propelled them to...

How can this dream improve the Force I am now working on?

Let me ask this question: is the kitchen where I'm nourished — or is it where I rush to-- as a forager?

Could it be I use the kitchen as a substance depot-- in order to boost my mood when I am having torpid times—

thinking or writing?

Food grabbed there lifts me up? It would be hard to deny that.

Therefore my Instinctive Force is improved if it learns from this dream not to rely on the kitchen for snacks-- when I am going there to be perked up.

But one must eat. The challenge is to learn to differentiate, so when going to the kitchen: I ask myself—Am I going in there to eat for nourishment or am I in there to fill my stomach for mood-medication?

I admit I have found myself using the kitchen as a boost to a tired mood. Perhaps you have done that as well.

So here we have gone through two incomplete dreams that helped us in spite of brevity.

I hope you're beginning to trust how powerful a teaching aid you have with dreams.

But always remember to ask those two questions. By asking them, you help yourself fetch answers and fresh thoughts from a slumbering mind that won't advise you willingly.

YOUR GOALS: TO BE SMOKE-FREE AND STRIVE TO BE THRIVING

DAY#16—TUESDAY—THE SEXUAL FORCE

IMPROVE YOUR SEXUAL FORCE THROUGH DREAMS—TO ACHIEVE YOUR GOALS!

WRITTEN UP DREAMS	*JOTTED DOWN DREAMS*

DAILY QUESTIONS TO ASK EACH OF THE DREAMS YOU HAVE:

#1.) WHAT'S MY EXPERIENCE WITH THIS DREAM FROM LAST NIGHT?

#2.) HOW DOES THIS DREAM IMPROVE THE FORCE I'M WORKING ON?

DAY SIXTEEN—TUESDAY—THE SEXUAL FORCE:

Dreams are often cast in perplexing enrichment. My guess is that they somehow know that if they spoke "straight out" --what they are all about-- we would not need to strive so hard.

The truth is that all prizes in life (yours and mine) come with a price tag— which is effort. If people con you that you can accomplish some objective with no real effort, hold them kindly in your eye and silently muse, "Then there must be a catch to it!."

I am no glutton for punishment, but I've learned everything worth treasuring takes real effort to achieve. Yet most people give up, because they've not learned their passion must be directed in undiminished work-force towards reaching the goal they're seeking.

I say all this to tell you that the two dreams that I dreamed last night were not easy for me to apply to the Force I'm working on.

It's critical to remember that whatever the dream: it's got to be thought of eventually as useful for improving that one Force.

First we experience the dream—begin to grasp its sense -- and then lastly we turn our attention to how it improves the Force we are on. It sometimes takes a lot of effort... and going back to the dream several times.

...And now let us turn to the two dreams that I dreamed:

•   *   *   *

Dream #1:"I recall a dream where some cousins came over. There was a car involved. I was impressed with what they did in coming over. My great nephew was also with them."

What sort of an experience did I have with this dream?

I was happy that they happened to come. I got pleasure out of whatever it was they'd done--visiting...I'm quite a bit older than they--and particularly my great nephew… He has energy, which I wouldn't mind…He loves to sing, as I do; and the boy has a bright look on his face that thrills folks.

Whenever I see a car in a dream, I need to refer back and recognize that there is a form of "mechanism of will" that is involved. You might ask me: "How is that? How do you know that's what "cars" are?" Specifically— many years past—I dreamed a dream, which said straight out, "A car is the "mechanism of the will."

Dreams infrequently may say the meaning of a word, which may not be what your dreams say. But for me, seeing a car will give me that tip. That doesn't mean that I always understand everything just because I know "car".

So how does this dream improve the Force I am working on? (It's the Sexual Force.)

Here's what I think improved this Force: It's natural when you get to be my age that you think Ye Olde Sexual Force has pretty much had it. But this dream asserts, "No!'

It's true you can't have the kind of sex you had when once young. But your Sex Force is there— openly there for youthfulness to visit you and be glad you can enjoy it.

Intimacy, too, can be had-- without having to delve into areas that have lost Nature's munificence. Merely holding one's spouse can have all the pleasure that one needs to be satisfied.

Let's now turn to the next dream that I had last night:

*   *   *   *

Dream #2: "'I seemed to be trying to focus on picking out the stuff I liked from the stuff I didn't on my plate of food. My father had just said when he married Mother he weighed one hundred and sixty-eight pounds. I had a hard time with thinking he weighed that much. He then turned to my mother nearby and said, "You know… when we were talking about when we married…Remember when I weighed one hundred and sixty-eight pounds?"'

What's my experience with last night's second dream?

Sometimes dreams show us and others-- not as we and they are but as examples of what we should be or shouldn't be…

I gather picking at my food is unsightly and unwelcome. It reminds me that when kids do that, the pros say it's a sign they have a problem that needs guidance.

Since Dad has become a quasi-guide (since his death), his weight must be a number I may need to emulate. That weight is slightly more than my weight now.

So in this dream I experience two behavior opposites: #1 -- picking food…#2-- weighing more.

How does this dream improve the Force I'm working on? (Recall: it's the Sexual Force.)

Rather than try to be circumspect about sex— almost wanting to refrain from it, I should not skimp on my approach, but rather experience it with fullness.

The phenomenon of my father weighing much more than he (a short-trim man) weighed… is how the dream recruits Dad to substitute a weight that he wants me to have —in place of the weight he has.

So not only is my Sexual Force being guided to gain a few more pounds, but also to retract from my concern to consume less. A dream like this can give one a sense of freedom— yet may take time getting used to. On the other hand, if one finds the way one has experienced a dream does not grant an improvement to the Force one's working on, then simply take a second look. It may be another grade of improvement has gone unnoticed and is now seen.

No dream should ever be used to harm oneself or cause distress to anyone else.

YOUR GOALS: TO BE SMOKE-FREE AND STRIVE TO BE THRIVING

DAY#17—WEDNESDAY—THE MOVING FORCE

IMPROVE YOUR MOVING FORCE THROUGH DREAMS—TO ACHIEVE YOUR GOALS!

WRITTEN UP DREAMS	*JOTTED DOWN DREAMS*

DAILY QUESTIONS TO ASK EACH OF THE DREAMS YOU HAVE:

#1.) WHAT'S MY EXPERIENCE WITH THIS DREAM FROM LAST NIGHT?

#2.) HOW DOES THIS DREAM IMPROVE THE FORCE I'M WORKING ON?

DAY SEVENTEEN—WEDNESDAY—THE MOVING FORCE

I invite you to read this long dream from last night. After you've looked at it, I'd like to describe a key point I thought the dream's about. It might surprise you what I thought.

   *   *   *   *

Dream #1: 'I recall a dream where I am visiting a fellow a bit older than I—rather successful in his line of work, and a renter or an owner (I'm not sure which) of two large suites of apartments. I had brought over with me— or met them there—several younger men whom apparently I knew. They were just starting out in their careers. As I waited for this man to file down something in his one suite (across the hall from his other one) I stepped out doors and noticed a row of quite dilapidated small houses with adjoining back yards where a few mutts lulled in sleep. I believe this guy had a cigarette in his hand at all times… Then, later, as another man came, the older gentleman introduced me to him—but quite surprisingly he told the new arriver that my name was not mine but someone else's. I said nothing to correct him—but I felt a bit put off. (Nothing's more insulting than calling a person by the wrong name.) We had just been discussing how one should comport oneself when one's meeting others. As I shook hands with the new man, I seemed to make a stout effort to shake his hand and move with great deference towards him.'

What's my experience with this first dream last night?

Let us take one theme at a time:

When this dream started out—I was expecting more from this guy, who affected me. His affluent aura certainly impressed me--as did his two apartment suites. But then things went south: how could dilapidated houses be so close to his home? And what about all those cigarettes he's smoking— during our long conversation?

But what really drove me to lower him in my esteem: this man failed to recall my name--instead: calling me someone else's name. There's no excuse… His eminent life style and prominence vanished when that happened.

So despite the dream having a high-toned look about it, I was disappointed.

How did this dream help to improve the Moving Force that I'm presently working on?

I think the main thrust of the dream was to emphasize how important it is in improving our behavior: to make sure we remember folks' names—whether it's when we introduce folks to others, or when we simply call them by name as we speak.

I have to think the takeaway from this dream was the way one's feelings can be stung when someone can't recall his name.

What's the thing-to-learn here? How can this Force improve?

I hope each of you answer that.

(By the way, please notice: in every dream I've dreamed -- thus far-- the guy smoking is shown to be unappealing. … Nothing's said directly— but his grossness is obvious.)

…Back to recalling names: I confess-- for many years—I had found I forgot names of people I'd just met or even sometimes old friends that I'd not seen in a while. I had tried all kinds of manuals, which aim at teaching folks how to remember— but I admit that none had really aided me.

I have shared my unableness with others, and I found that nine out of ten of them have the same problem I had. It's our common default.

I can only advise all ninth graders to make sure that you are always trying to remember people's names –whether old friends or new ones.

If I had to suggest to people-- just starting out in careers-- a pretty prime goal: it would be to just remember the names of everyone that chance brings to them..

There is truly nothing that you can tell people that ranks

higher than saying their names as you meet them or as you come across them. Such a skill will surely help you thrive greatly in your life.--no matter how smart or how un-smart you happen to be. Remembering names will help put you at the top of the group of successful folks.

Here's a disturbing truth: If we forget names, it's probably from our not being interested in folks. (And those folks may sense that.) So by working hard to become interested in folks: we will recall their names.

In other words, let's train ourselves to be interested—whenever we meet folks. That helps our lives to be thriving.-

Now I had two short dreams, which may be putting me in my place—as you might soon grasp:

* * * *

Dream #2:'I recall taking out a quarter and with it in hand quickly acting like a prestidigitator—moving the coin across my right hand and ending up with the quarter falling to the pavement—making a tinkling sound. An onlooker picked it up—but I made light of retrieving it—as if dropping it showed no failure.'

What's my experience with last night's second dream?

It's a form of paradox that I have to concede in this dream: I looked like a dunce in the way I was failing with that coin.

A magician can make a coin vanish— not really—but before our eyes, it looks as if he is able to achieve that.

All of my hand-waving didn't accomplish that feat; it showed me failing terribly. The paradox is, however: I really didn't feel any shame or failure.

How does this dream improve the Force that I am working on?

Am I some kind of fake-- as I try to do fancy tricks? (Presumably with dreams?) It almost looks that way. But maybe—just maybe-- I am admitting to all folks who may be reading this: that I am not trying to have them believe that I can make a coin disappear. I know that is really a fake.

I'm simply proving to folks that I can't do tricks... All I'm trying to reveal to them is that I can't make a coin appear to vanish. That would be plain- cheating on them.

(I hope you follow the logic I'm expressing.)

I am not like a magician. As a matter of fact, by FAILING in the trick, I validate I WON'T CHEAT YOU.

You see, I won't make coins vanish truly by my hand gyrations and fake magic. All I can do--and I want you to learn this for yourself-- is that like all others-- I can only strive to work with my dreams on the level where I am now standing;

And that's good enough for what I seek to achieve— keeping you far from cigarettes and pointing you towards a life that becomes thriving.

Maybe this dream is close to an admonishment not to try magic to make coins vanish, but—with no magic—to gain your trust that I can only be above board-- helping you gain guidance from dreams.

Now, lastly, let's look at the third dream from last night:

•   *   *   *

Dream #3: 'I recall a little girl tugging on her mom's long black dress—till part of it came off in the child's hands. I was astonished how the mother did not get too upset.'

What's my experience with this third dream last night?

I really sensed the mother halfway expected the child to behave as she did... But as I watched the child tug, I found myself hoping the mother would not let the child get it all.

But it happened; and yet the mother was not naked. She had on something white that lay underneath....Perhaps the mother let the child have her own way.

How does this dream improve the Force that I'm now working on?

I identified with the mother; I made you the child. I'll tell you why I made that connection right now: The dream smartly has revealed you-- tugging at my skirt to try to get attention away from me and onto you. Maybe you've a sense I am spending too much time on my dreams and none on your dreams.

But here's my point in the way I am doing this: (And this dream lets me explain it.) I want you to see how I am working with dreams.

Try not to tug at my ego— but merely accept what I am experiencing as a method you can work with.

How else could I teach you how to do what I do--other than to show you straight-out.

This dream does help me to improve the Moving Force by bringing me fresh awareness of how your patience may be strained over my dreams. I'll try to keep that in my mind.

And I ask you to take your eyes off of just me and focus on how you can dream.

YOUR GOALS: TO BE SMOKE-FREE AND STRIVE TO BE THRIVING

DAY#18—THURSDAY—THE FEELING FORCE

IMPROVE YOUR FEELING FORCE THROUGH DREAMS—TO ACHIEVE YOUR GOALS!

WRITTEN UP DREAMS	*JOTTED DOWN DREAMS*

DAILY QUESTIONS TO ASK EACH OF THE DREAMS YOU HAVE:

#1.) WHAT'S MY EXPERIENCE WITH THIS DREAM FROM LAST NIGHT?

#2.) HOW DOES THIS DREAM IMPROVE THE FORCE I'M WORKING ON?

DAY EIGHTEEN—THURSDAY—THE FEELING FORCE

Let me share a tip, which at first glance may appear plain witless and without value:

When you awaken from one of your durations of night sleep —in front of the dawn— and your foremost regret is that you've had no dreams: rest quietly and ponder, 'PAUSE'.

I don't know what force there is in that word, but quite often a dream drifts upwards to mind, and slowly you will sense it as one you've dreamed.

The following dreams that I had were recalled in that way.

(Before I thought of "PAUSE", I was empty-handed with dreams. I literally could not recall anything. Then I thought, 'PAUSE' --stoutly within-- and each of these two dreams floated across my mind.)

Here's the first one as it appeared:

*   *   *   *

Dream #1: 'I am at my old steel company. A fellow comes in, as I work at the shop desk with my former boss. The fellow asked for me to take care of some need he had—but either he saw I was busy with something else or I told him that I was—so he said he'd return.. Meanwhile my former boss kibitzed with him, which proved to be an interruption to me anyway. Then I see another customer in a black pick up pulling into the driveway. All of this made me feel quite upset with the fact that I was not able to control the events that were taking place.'

What's my experience with this first dream last night?

Even as I experienced the above-mentioned dream, shame came into my heart. How could I be so arrogant with people who wished to do business with me? How dare I dare to feel this way? Am I a spoiled child? Or am I so rich or rude that I could let myself act this way with such selfishness? There is really no good excuse for my behaving so.

So how does this dream help to improve my Feeling Force?

It causes me to see me-- as I used to behave inwardly— when I could not control work-interruptions. The fact that I'm dreaming of a time that's long gone drives me to think I'm still the same— if any similar situation arose.

I no longer own my steel firm, but suppose my time would become usurped with folks who want to talk about this book? Would I inwardly sense resentment with being obliged to spend my time with them? If I have that feeling, then I'm in the wrong place. If I can't find a way to be thrilled with folks' interest in what I am doing, then I should not get so involved.

…Suppose people rush up to me with questions about this book: am I going to push them away or welcome them?

I think the answer is: I'll surely welcome them. Why them, and not those in the dream? Because I have a real passion for helping ninth graders like you keep from smoking…

The truth is: I had no pure passion for being a businessman -- involved with steel. That whole career was brought on from necessity.

So the message here is: don't be in a business that you have little passion for. I know, sometimes, that can't be helped. But when one feels as I do (as shown in the dream) it's important to note the truth and either determine to change one's attitude or make plans to do something else.

Some people are able to delegate those parts of a business they do not like, so they can work on those parts that they truly love.

…Dreams like this do work as a shock in revealing one's faults and informing one that now's the time to seek change to thrive.

So often, I think a person starts smoking in order to calm his angry nerves and get drugged up to deal with feelings this dream shows. But smoking is no thriving-fix.

…Now in a different vein, let's view the other dream, which

contains concrete advice.

*   *   *   *

Dream #2: 'I dreamed I was standing before an audience talking about my present work of trying to help ninth graders stay away from smoking. I tell them I had tried getting present-day folks who already smoked to stop—with another book-- yet believed what I was now doing—writing a book to keep ninth graders from smoking—might be much more effective. When I stopped speaking, I asked for any hands with some questions. An odd feeling I had—as I spoke—was I had decided much earlier I was not going to talk about this new project until I had completed it.'

This dream held an experience that I mainly enjoyed. When a dream confirms what we are in fact doing, I think there is an acceptance on the part of the dream that what we are doing is in line with what our Unconscious believes that we should do. A harmony's shown to exist between our conscious and our unconscious segments. If that happens to you, rejoice.

If your Unconscious does not even acknowledge what you're doing, it may be a sign that something you are doing is not quite right. That's the second reason dreams help. They can not only tell you what you should achieve; but-- through silence-- they can signal that what you are doing may not be right for you. This dream shows I'm on the right track.

One concrete thought that calls for consideration is when I muse: 'I decided I would not discuss my project till completed.' I've heard folks say, "Once you begin blabbing about your plans, they fly out the window, and you're left with less energy for pursuing those plans." In other words, my words might take the place of my efforts.

How does this dream improve the Force I'm working on?

Well…contrary to the last dream, I have confirmation that my actions are right. You may state, "Big deal! How's that great?" But we're lonely hunters when it comes to living. It's good when folks applaud our work, yet even as thrilling is when dreams confirm it. We begin to get the feeling that we're on the right track— and no one can intrude and convince us of something else.

The world is full of folks saying "NO!" to other folks who now thirst for achievement. It's tempting for folks "B" to be turned off by "NO!" Yet, achievers have to bear "NO's". And you can be sure that every single thing you heed about you— start from the floor you are now standing on and let your eyes travel all the way up to sky-filled planes-- and you can bet real bucks that most of it was first greeted with "NO!". Had the folks who were trying to achieve their goals stopped with those "NO'S", we would still be inhabiting forests and glens without any modern comforts.

As I said up in the front of this day's dream work, without thinking the word 'PAUSE', both of those dreams would be lost for good; and I would not have the benefit of their worth.

I also want to share two more dreams I had this past night… I share them not for my sake but to keep guiding you towards your own dream involvement and life development.

(There's no limit to what dreams yield.)

*   *   *   *

Dream #3: 'A weather forecast with the TV screen full of colored blotches …and an unseen announcer saying: 'A cold spell in the quite near future.' (I wonder what that is about.)'

Of course, weather forecasts cast less than what often shows up; but--in a dream--it makes practical sense to hear them out and ponder what they mean. Here I'm a bit puzzled with all of the colored blotches. They would have been cities in real life weather casts. I didn't quite know what to think…

Now a cold spell forecast isn't very cheerful. But better to be warned than not…

How would this dream improve the Force I'm working on?

Our lives are part of Nature's plan. The weather, too, is part of the very same plan. So if we have a cold spell, well … our task is to make sure we stay warm at all times—outwardly and inwardly, too.

So I take this dream as a thoughtful warning that my Feeling Force should be disposed towards a cold reception of my project in the near future. My chore is mainly to keep myself sheltered from this cold and always stay well-fed and suitably clothed.

We will never be ones to dictate the weather; nor can we call out a command to the Powers-That-Be for only fair weather. Dreams remind us we're not in charge as far as the weather or how our projects fare. But we are in charge of how the weather works inside of our own feelings; and there we can learn to make it just right.

…Onto the fourth and last dream that I dreamed last night.

This started out as satire:

*   *   *   *

Dream #4: 'Someone calls a doctor; and several hours later a guy pulls up in a black van, emerges dressed in workman's clothes-- and from the street calls out, "Did someone call a doctor?" I'm amused about his dress code and, moreover, that he is making a house call. Later, as he sat in the house he had come to (I'm a visitor there) he explained he was deaf. I was astounded that he could do his work with just lips and gestures. He said something about The New York Times making a complaint that questioned why so many headlines appeared in his article. He had told them that all the headlines he had inserted in the piece simply served as needed fillers.'

If you could have seen this guy emerge from his van and then call out, you might have laughed. Was this whole thing a joke? Nevertheless, someone did call for the doctor.

Really, my experience with this dream seemed unsettled. It was absurd and serious.

I recall feeling at the end of the dream—when he talked about headline fillers— that perhaps he's bringing up a topic that I had been thinking about for the text I was now typing. With all of the print here, might I not need some fillers, too?

As is often the case in dreams, something that you as a reader may not discern can be very helpful to the person dreaming. That's why only dreamers grasp dreams.

Another thing that I experienced was the change I had in my opinion of this so-called doctor. Before, I just smirked at his appearance. Now I had great respect for the fact that he had circumvented his handicap of deafness with immense perseverance in mastering the lips and gestures of folks he treated.

How does this dream help to improve my Feeling Force?

People can strike us as quite strange and yet gradually grow into fresh greatness when we begin to respect them.

Maybe the guy was no more a doctor than I am, but he did show up, share his life experiences with us… and for all I know, somehow, he came to show me something about fillers' necessity as well as how such a fellow succeeds.

The immediacy of these dreams is that we use them right now to improve the Force that we're working on. The accumulation of one dream on top of others should gradually grow our lives until we thrive from all we've learned and never smoke.

[61]

YOUR GOALS: TO BE SMOKE-FREE AND STRIVE TO BE THRIVING

DAY#19—FRIDAY—THE THINKING FORCE

IMPROVE YOUR THINKING FORCE THROUGH DREAMS—TO ACHIEVE YOUR GOALS!

WRITTEN UP DREAMS	*JOTTED DOWN DREAMS*

DAILY QUESTIONS TO ASK EACH OF THE DREAMS YOU HAVE:

#1.) WHAT'S MY EXPERIENCE WITH THIS DREAM FROM LAST NIGHT?

#2.) HOW DOES THIS DREAM IMPROVE THE FORCE I'M WORKING ON?

DAY NINETEEN—FRIDAY—THE THINKING FORCE

Here's a thought I want to explore with you right now:

How do you act when you just may find yourself with more dreams than you've time to devote? How much of your time can you spend on the dreams that you dream? Fifteen minutes... perhaps, thirty minutes?

After a time you may begin to think that dreams are like a-corns: thousands fall from above. How few acorns--on the ground—will ever turn into oaks?

Yes... Nature teems with potential.

My advice is to act the best you can with the time that you have. You may find—once you've locked into this book—your dream work will become like a hobby; and you'll commence spending all the free time you're able to summon.

I don't want you ever to think the feat's overwhelming---with the time that you have. My belief is—when you're earnest-- whatever time you give dreams will be sufficient to achieve the goals here for you: keep from smoking and live a life that is thriving. Of course, a life that's thriving must be a work in progress-- but at least you'll begin with what you'll get out of this book.

So let's begin with the first dream I had last night. Please note--when I say "last night"—I am also including hours in the morning before you wake to live your day.

*   *   *   *

Dream #1: 'An uncle appears at noon one day. We look out of our second story window and see him getting out of a Cadillac he apparently had just purchased. It looked second-hand to me. Soon he comes upstairs and sits down in a chair in my room and wants to know what we have for him to eat. Sensing his wrong, he proposes we go out for something. He thinks he'd like to get breakfast. It is lunchtime for us.'

What's my experience with this first dream last night?

One point I want to mention here: when you have a dream that touches on past events, it's good to deal with that time first. In this dream, this uncle of mine was my hero. He stayed single for a long time and always seemed to live a more exciting life than his brother, my dear father. Dad was a successful businessman, but his brother travelled and partied and lawyered politically. I always liked hearing his tales when he visited us.

In this dream, I must be about twelve years of age. At seventy-nine, here I am dreaming of him-- long dead-- with a different take.

What could be my experience with this first dream last night?

There's no admiration as there once was. He strikes me as a guy who barges in whenever he cares to, making demands or then switching and offering favors where none is now needed.

So how does this dream improve the Force I am working on —today—my Thinking Force.?

I do not need to have people in my life that surround me with their selfishness. I should never be overwhelmed by another's lifestyle. I'm secure in my own.

What I hope this dream does for you is to stir you up to think about your own self. Even though at your age you will be impressionable with what others might do: always work on your own life force.

So often people start smoking thanks to their lack of self-esteem. Smoking's for them what my uncle was for me—an outlet to a more exciting life (as "grown-up") while yet so young. With its rank worldliness, smoking ignites "mature posture" in youth. Seen from afar-- you'll note, however, there is much ugliness in smoking and much pretense in young people.

Let me share some more dreams that I had this past night:

*   *   *   *

Dream #2: 'A woman who seems to be an assistant of mine goes out and on her own buys a refrigerator. I ask what it costs. She says, "Two hundred dollars a week." I get upset: 'Why pay by the week?' In the dream, I could handle paying at once and avoiding any interest involved in the commitment of a weekly payment. The lady says she decided on one model from one store over a model from another store. Then one more worker who's employed by me comes over with a serious face and says, "I see that you are spending a lot of time as you review a management decision. But you've got to deal with one other issue that's urgent right away." He takes me over to a table where a huge pastry pan is loaded to the gills with some sort of well-powdered pastries. He explains these are all going to a company that's having a party. I'm slightly taken aback since that firm's not even our customer—but then sense that perhaps such an involvement with this large tray of pastries will help us woo the firm favorably.'

What's my experience with last night's second dream?

It strikes me my experience with this dream is a sort of cautionary tale. It teaches me that it's vital for me to be involved with these two employees. (I've questioned such.) Surely a fault of mine was not taking an interest in what folks were doing whom I employed. Maybe it's wearisome-- what I'm obliged to bear--but it's part of running a firm.

How long does it take to question an employee on a purchase or ruminate over whether one should generate new business by sending a firm some sweets? Maybe the whole thing would take less than an hour.

Does my response have much effect? The one who bought the large refrigerator learns that I don't want her buying stuff without remembering a principle I have: Always to buy items with no involvement in paying interest. That shows her that we're solvent and quite prudent. The other fellow learns or finds his thoughts confirmed that I don't mind spending money in an effort to gain a major customer. (That's not spending; that's investing.) It's not a bad thing for me to see myself in two roles that I need to provide.

How does this dream improve my Thinking Force, which I am working on?

I teach myself something that I never clearly knew in business. Maybe at some time another business will occur with me so invested. Then I may be better involved.

Here is the third dream that I dreamed in the past night: (Often the dead are in our dreams.)

•   *   *   *

Dream #3:'My mother has started out saying I was to get over ten thousand dollars in some refund from the U.S. Government—and she added there was something that she had expensed that she wanted me to pay her for.
(No idea what this might be.)'

What's my experience with this third dream last night?

This is so far from what my mom would ever do that it really does puzzle me. Here, too, Mother's been gone for years.

Why do we dream about people who are deceased? People have been pondering that for longer than we know. I don't really think that deceased people can contact us. That doesn't mean that their spirits aren't within us. And I would not attempt to talk anyone who believes that I am mistaken into thinking I am correct. The truth may be that no one's belief applies to all. Each of us may have our own. And I'm of the belief that whatever helps you carry on in this world—without wishing to kill folks who don't believe as you do—is fine with me. But my thought is: we dream of the deceased because our Unconscious wants them to be part of our growth.

Sometimes--as in the last dream--the person is there to force us to see a new truth. Now-- in this dream—even though my mother, here, is not remotely like my mother, somehow her presence is needed to help me grow. In other words, staffing this dream with Mom in it, improves the Force I'm working on.

The first thought is that money should never be coveted. Yes, one should work for it. But if cash comes out of the blue, one should not become so self-absorbed that he's not willing to share it with "Mother". "Mother" might stand for things that have nourished one's self. That makes good sense to me right now.

…You may say, "Hey, you are making up that meaning!" (You're quite welcome to that complaint.) My response is that you should turn to your own dreams and go through the steps as I have First, experience what the dream brings to your mind. Then ask yourself: "How am I helped in improving the Force that I'm now working on?"

See what you come up with for you. That's really the whole point of my doing my dreams: to stimulate you to do yours.

Here's the fourth dream that I happened to dream last night (from sublime to ridiculous…)

   *   *   *   *

Dream #4: 'Several folks discuss their impression of some woman's bosoms. Apparently they had espied them in some way as she was in private taking care of some need. I ask how big they were—I think—sort of going along with the idea of always following stuff like this with curious questions. I made a big gesture with my two hands—as if representing the size of a full-grown watermelon.'

What could be my experience with this voyeuristic dream I, a dream guy, had?

I'm naturally appalled with folks spying on ladies when they're privately engaged. That crosses the line without doubt; but having heard about this amply gifted soul, I was simply using a tact that I have found very valuable in my relations with all forms of folks.

There's even a book out that I happened to read, which talks about how important it is to be willing to show you're curious with questions when you engage folks.

Was I really dead set in learning how large the lady's bosoms happened to be? Hardly—but honestly, asking questions is a way to maintain our connection with people. At some point the topic ought to turn into something more uplifting.

But to ask: how does this dream help improve the Force I'm working on, I would say it reinforces what the book states on every page: be curious. It helps you learn, and it helps other folks know you're interested in what they say.

Psychiatrists may elucidate: when we ask a passerby: "How you doing?"... We are letting that fair fellow know that we're making effort to be bonded in some way to him.

However, if that guy would then stop and tell you all the ills that now afflict him, you might regret that you took the time to ask him.

...And--at last—here is the fifth dream:

• * * *

Dream #5: 'A group of us has been given the big task of putting into some drawing the many factors that have touched upon our days' life. I seemed to have a difficult time executing this task. I started off a couple of times with various representations of the power of the strong Forces that come into our lives. At the end of the time allotted to this work I hadn't done anything that appeared tangible—while I latched onto a few drawings by folks who impressed me. A woman came over and showed me how one thing could represent toilets. I made a mental commitment I would work on this task whenever I had some spare time. One guy had done a quite impressive drawing. At the bottom he inserted a label with his name on it: "T.Ryan". When up, I thought the name stood for 'T-ryin'. Someone else's drawing consisted of a bunch of twenty-four by thirty-six sheets all taped together. That struck me as what one could present on stage to others.'

What might I have experienced with this fifth dream last night?

I was not confident in my talent for making a drawing that had in it the Forces that touched down on my life each and every day. I just stumbled around with crayon and paper... Maybe I could do better now. But then, I couldn't put Forces down on paper...like I was hand- cuffed in my mind.

How could this dream improve my Thinking Force that I'm now working on?

Well...it's one thing to talk about Forces; and it's another to start practicing drawing Forces. Might this improve the Force that I'm now working on?

Will I really start this task now? Will I do it when I have spare time to do it? I will try to.

I don't always follow what dreams advise and do them all the time. But reminding myself does help.

Like so much in my life: I always have a choice. I can choose to neglect wisdom that dreams have given me— or I can obey them.

The secret sauce is attempting to execute them when I really don't want to. It's that friction between 'yes' and 'no' that creates the part in us that develops--when we propel ourselves to act.

YOUR GOALS: TO BE SMOKE-FREE AND STRIVE TO BE THRIVING

DAY#20—SATURDAY—THE HIGHER FEELING FORCE

IMPROVE YOUR HIGHER FEELING FORCE THROUGH DREAMS—TO ACHIEVE YOUR GOALS!

WRITTEN UP DREAMS	*JOTTED DOWN DREAMS*

DAILY QUESTIONS TO ASK EACH OF THE DREAMS YOU HAVE:

#1.) WHAT'S MY EXPERIENCE WITH THIS DREAM FROM LAST NIGHT?

#2.) HOW DOES THIS DREAM IMPROVE THE FORCE I'M WORKING ON?

DAY TWENTY—SATURDAY—THE HIGHER FEELING FORCE

Occasionally you may have a dream that makes terrific sense-- while you dream it-- but then when you wake up and write down the dream, and later begin to dwell on it, you find that its meaning is quite hard to detect— or at least hard to sense how it improves the Force that you're currently working on. That's how I feel right now as I ponder the first dream that I had during last night:

•   *   *   *

Dream #1: 'I dreamed of a TV interview that was held with a behind-the-scene movie director of a film that showed a railroad scene. It was very interesting to see how they took a scene that had to be filled-- only for a moment-- with the looks of a train running on a track, which had to have hundreds of holes drilled to give its true effect to the audience of viewers. I was amazed with all of this.'

What's my experience with this first dream last night?

I recognize the source of the dream—from a film trailer I had seen recently…That trailer showed the intense work and dedication that went into making the railroad tracks look as authentic as possible; and the scene was only going to last for a few short minutes. That is what I call an incredible passion towards making a film impressive.

How does this dream improve the Force I'm working on? (It's the Higher Feeling Force now.)

If filmmakers can spend so much time and effort just to achieve a few moments of authenticity-- showing a railroad track-- how much more should I be willing to spend helping young folks learn to use their dreams to keep from smoking?

…Look what's happened: whereas I started out unable to see the meaning in this dream: Just by my typing and expressing this inability— something kicked in, and voila! I have just now found meaning where I hadn't before.

This is the sort of good fortune that I trust you will find as you wrestle with dreams and willingly give yourself time to pin down an insight that will help you improve the Force that you are working on.

There is so much going on between our Conscious and Unconscious that we don't see: until we give the two some free rein to connect-- as we indulge in expression.

…Let's go to the next dream, which I'm not so proud of— at least before I work on it:

*   *   *   *

Dream #2: 'I'm sneaking French kisses with a woman I've known. After each kiss, we peer around an open door of the refrigerator in the kitchen where we're carrying on. I am wearing light blue pajamas with the leg lengths so long I turn up the ends.'

What's my experience with last night's second dream?

If the legs are too long for my comfort, the chances are this dream, itself, is not comfortable for me to have. But the forbidden scene makes the dream exciting.

In my younger days-- before I married-- there was something erotic about my sneaking kisses with a woman close to where others were--but far enough away they probably wouldn't see us. There's that adrenalin high from this kind of sex that some folks seek-- like it's a drug.

How does this dream improve the Force I'm working on?

Sometimes, I've found that dreams grant an experience that should never encourage us. Nevertheless, people often use a dream like this as advice they should act on. I believe that we should never act on a dream that would end up hurting someone.

Since I'm married, such an action would spiritually or existentially hurt my wife. So what it shows me is that any thought on this level of living should surely be steered away from. (I've gotten delight in derring-do without my having to deal with penalties.)

To summarize: this dream lets me act in bad faith but, hopefully, then teaches me it's not something that can make my life thriving..

Realizing my moral code improves the Higher Force I am now working on. Such is the rare genius of dreams.

There are a lot of folks who might cheat on their spouse— often owning a plethora of reasons why they might— without ever having the advantage of hearing what their dreams might say of it. If they had benefit of dreams' worthy inner resource, they might be able to gain moral character and free themselves from wrong doing.

Is it possible that their dreams might console them and agree with their cheat-actions? I don't know that answer— but maybe rationale does exist that I don't know of.

…I believe much smoking occurs when folks choose to satisfy their lusts and then sense keen discomfort within that leads them to smoking.

Smoking can salve a lot of guilt. But how much wiser a person becomes who can use his dreams as true arbiters for his moral conduct in all aspects of life. And dreams are free for the asking.

YOUR GOALS: TO BE SMOKE-FREE AND STRIVE TO BE THRIVING

DAY#21—SUNDAY—THE HIGHER THINKING FORCE

IMPROVE YOUR HIGHER THINKING FORCE THROUGH DREAMS—TO ACHIEVE YOUR GOALS!

WRITTEN UP DREAMS	*JOTTED DOWN DREAMS*

DAILY QUESTIONS TO ASK EACH OF THE DREAMS YOU HAVE:

#1.) WHAT'S MY EXPERIENCE WITH THIS DREAM FROM LAST NIGHT?

#2.) HOW DOES THIS DREAM IMPROVE THE FORCE I'M WORKING ON?

DAY TWENTY-ONE—SUNDAY—THE HIGHER THINKING FORCE

Are you ever in a hurry to get away? Never mind where—never mind why... Often it indicates a reluctance to be involved with folks in some manner.

This first dream last night shows me in that frame of mind:

• * * *

Dream #1:'I am at my old steel company. Workers have gone home. It's late afternoon—becoming evening. There's some fellow in the steel yard. Then three others appear. I'm intent on leaving. The one guy says that some restaurant is offering free food—meat and such. I and an associate in business think about trying there—though I was not so gung-ho, since I am a vegan. I'm in a hurry to get going—even with the other men standing around. I start off carrying a long twig, and--as I walk--I run it along the outer growth of a quite large evergreen tree. Now one man says out loud of me: "He really does not mess around."

What's my experience with this first dream last night?

Seeing how I am with walk-ins, it's quite clear from this dream that I never had much passion for new steel customers.

True, it's time to go home— but several folks come in… Shouldn't I—as owner—welcome them, ask how they're doing, engage them, thank them for coming, and ask how can I help?

My passion isn't there. My attitude is such as to reveal a man who is never going to be open when the breaks come. Good luck's blocked by such impatience.

Is it fresh news to me I once acted this way when I owned a steel company? Not really.... But to dream this now seems to warn me I should make sure I have the right passion—if I ever have a new business.

And furthermore: how do I feel when I hear a guy say of me, "He really does not mess around." (Not much praise, here.)

The thought that struck me as I wrote down the dream was how defiant it was for me to run a twig along the outside of a tree-- instead of just "beating around the bush--" which as you may know is an idiom for someone who doesn't get to the point (in business).

People want salesmen to take some time to get to know them. They don't appreciate someone who just acts out, "WHAT DO YOU WANT?" ('GET TO THE POINT!')

One of the exciting rewards of dream-writing is detecting imagery that makes you recall an idiom you have learned. Such connections bring you that much closer to the genius, which is revealed in dreams.

As you enrich your language-life with idioms, you will find yourself detecting them in dreams...The more idioms you have learned, the greater chance you'll have to really experience a dream's true sense.

Now how does this dream help to improve the Force I am working on?

It brings to mind the way I've often lacked the curiosity to engage with folks of all stripes. I do admire souls who converse naturally.

How much more do I learn—seeing myself in a dream— blunt and unfriendly-- than if someone sermonized—pointing out my wrong behavior. And regardless of how I feel from a dream such as this, I should always thank it for helping me improve. No sermon can ever help us as much as we, ourselves... through the use of our dreams.

Let us now look at the next dream:

•   *   *   *

Dream #2: 'My son and another guy head out, and I try to figure out how long some brace is going to take to fabricate. I see and call to them on the parking lot.'

What's my experience with this next dream last night?

I suspect there is more detail in this dream, but I failed to take in what that was. Nevertheless, I make it a practice to use any information I find in the dream that I have just dreamed.

What comes to mind when I experience this brief dream that I had during the night?

Well… I'd say I'm trying to estimate while the two boys go off to just be boys. Shouldn't I possibly be more interested in being with them than hiding behind some work that might be postponed till later?

As a parent shouldn't I be wary about working when opportunity presents itself to be with my son and one of his friends? That's the question that came to mind as I pondered this dream. I'd say I was using work as an excuse to avoid spending time with those two.

How does this dream improve the Force I'm working on?

When it's between working on "work" or engaging with folks (especially a son) I think I should select my son. Of course, it's true—sometimes--we need to spend time with material challenges—like figuring how long it takes to fabricate stuff. But we should not use a challenge-- like that example—as an excuse to ponder alone over work and avoid valuable chances to build relationships.

Now I will be candid with you: When I first started to "experience" this dream, I didn't get much out of it. And I want you to know that can happen to you. Yet, don't give up. Don't turn away--right off the bat-- and think, "I get nothing from this." Give your mind a chance to help you. There is so much treasure within your mind that you've failed to perceive; and here with dreams you'll have the greatest of opportunities to start to find your mind's potential.

YOUR GOALS: TO BE SMOKE-FREE AND STRIVE TO BE THRIVING

DAY#22—MONDAY—THE INSTINCTIVE FORCE

IMPROVE YOUR INSTINCTIVE FORCE THROUGH DREAMS—TO ACHIEVE YOUR GOALS!

WRITTEN UP DREAMS	JOTTED DOWN DREAMS

DAILY QUESTIONS TO ASK EACH OF THE DREAMS YOU HAVE:

#1.) WHAT'S MY EXPERIENCE WITH THIS DREAM FROM LAST NIGHT?

#2.) HOW DOES THIS DREAM IMPROVE THE FORCE I'M WORKING ON?

DAY TWENTY-TWO—MONDAY—THE INSTINCTIVE FORCE

I had only one dream that I could consciously remember, and it went like this:

 *   *   *   *

Dream #1: 'My parents are giving a summer party, and I arrive and enjoy meeting and greeting all the folks. I recognize them all but hardly call any by name. One fellow shows me a photo taken at my father's steel firm. It was taken in Dad's private office; and the photo featured my dad head on: he's sitting at his desk with his hat on—and in the picture you can see my two feet on the desk without seeing any other portion of me. I have on soft leather strollers. Dad had his feet and part of his legs on the desk. This was during business hours.'

What's my experience with this one dream last night?

I must have been in my twenties when the party took place. I don't recall any such party, but--in the dream—it all seemed delightful--- with my parents enjoying a period when they were young and well; and Dad was in the midst of his success. There was a joy all around me.

The photo, also, was not something that was shot—although—in the dream--it surely depicted a life style of taking things easy during a day at the office. Business must have been so good we were slumping in our seats with nothing to do. I even had on the kind of strollers I would never wear at a steel concern. But all in all there was joy in my heart-- sort of like a child who knows no struggles.

…Now, how would this dream help to improve the Force I am working on? I think it's great when joy is all around, but—when the joy simply comes from being sheltered from truth-- it seems a bit fruitless.

The dream is forcing me to recognize and keep in mind that the true path to joy is doing something that comes from within— which not only serves one's deepest needs, but also directs one's acts towards the welfare of other folks. Then when one finds joy, it's based on a connection to Nature's plan— not selfishness.

The joyful sense for me is now: for this one time, I am doing dream work for this book that well resonates with my sense of thriving in my life.

As I review these dreams-- and while I comment-- I'm feeling that I am on the right path. It is a sense that I hope you will find as you work on your dreams.

People can earn all the money, take all the trips, have all the material gains and still feel that something's lacking within their private souls. They'll never admit it, unless their fraught egos cave in; and they are desperate for somebody's succor.

But it's not for you or me to watch when that might happen and waste time in gossip. Too much time is spent hungering after information about folks in the news. Better that we spend energy developing the skills and capacities that we innately possess right now.

So this dream I just had strikes me as improving my gratefulness for where I am— for fondly recalling how my parents once were— but currently realizing that the joy I felt in that dream can still exist-- yet on a plane that's loftier.

I don't wear loafers to work at my father's firm— where I seemed to loaf in the dream-- but type-- with my hands and mind—the thoughts that come forth--as I work to utilize dreams.

I will also add that I would wager no one starts smoking if the work she does comes from deep within her. I suspect new smokers seek a false joy found in smoking.

There's a belief by some that our bodies obey the frustrations held in our minds. If we "can't stand something": our legs may obey with a hardship that makes standing tough. If we're "fed up with stuff": our stomach may obey with hardships of indigestion. And if we can't reverse the negative feelings that our life has imposed on us: we might take up smoking to medicate or tamp down those feelings with nicotine. Whatever cause there might be that enters the mind and effects the body's actions… dreams can often help us come to terms with the cause-- so life for us becomes thriving.

YOUR GOALS: TO BE SMOKE-FREE AND STRIVE TO BE THRIVING

DAY#23—TUESDAY—THE SEXUAL FORCE

IMPROVE YOUR SEXUAL FORCE THROUGH DREAMS—TO ACHIEVE YOUR GOALS!

WRITTEN UP DREAMS	JOTTED DOWN DREAMS

DAILY QUESTIONS TO ASK EACH OF THE DREAMS YOU HAVE:

#1.) WHAT'S MY EXPERIENCE WITH THIS DREAM FROM LAST NIGHT?

#2.) HOW DOES THIS DREAM IMPROVE THE FORCE I'M WORKING ON?

DAY TWENTY-THREE—TUESDAY—THE SEXUAL FORCE

    *   *   *   *

Dream #1: 'I recall a series of events that ended with some degree of harmony. Folks were sitting—speaking kindly to each other.'

What's my experience with this first dream last night?

Here is a dream that I could not remember in any detail; and yet I could write down the sense I got from it. And that sense was a lot of good feeling from it.

The goal we are striving for in the dream work we do is to attain harmony in all of our Forces. It strikes me here that at least in this dream-- in this Force—rare harmony has been achieved.

How does this dream improve the Force I'm working on?

Just to spend a few moments in quiet reflection of a dream can leave you with a harmony that's most welcome… and particularly in the Sexual Force-- which in our age has become—for some--a dysfunctional factor through early years.

The emphasis some give this Force can often outweigh all of the emphases they give the other six big Forces.

So whenever we have a dream that ushers in some harmony … it's a blessing.

And anytime we can fill our minds and hearts with such harmony helps us touch the depth of thriving we yearn for in our regular day-to-day lives. (That's worth a try.)

Here is the second dream that came to me last night:

    *   *   *   *

Dream #2: 'I'm visiting my mom and son and having a conversation. My mother is concerned that what I have been doing for a long period, I've suddenly stopped and have gone into some other activities. I said, 'Well, the question is, is this change good or bad? I think it's good… and you don't know.'… Later an old friend talks with another old friend. The one needs guidance on some matter, and it has partly to do with a pair of long trousers. The one guy tells the other that he should take them to some place and once there it will be on the street, and we can then have a better chance to see what he ought to do...Now someone comes in and covers the bed I'm in with a light green blanket. (Is this some idiom for putting the matter to rest?)'

What's my experience with last night's second dream?

Before I say...it seems that this is possibly a good time for me to repeat I've been involved with dream work for at least fifty plus years.

What I am bringing to your attention and teaching you may not be the sort of "knowledge" psychologists or certified psychiatrists would tend to ratify. (And that's as it should be.)

Yet, my method's brought me a lot of health and happiness — and pointed me in new directions towards a thriving life.

Hopefully, at your age, this short digression here will get you to think: there are a lot of paths for helping people fulfill their lives. Professionals have theirs; and I have a less travelled one that I sincerely hope helps you: 1.) not take up smoking and 2.) learn to live a life that becomes thriving.

Here's something else I'd like to say: Psychiatry started out with Sigmund Freud who treated many neurotic folks. Through them, he discovered so much in their psyche and in their dreams revolved around sexual obsessions.

With my method, I have not found that the sexual stuff's much more self-defeating than any of the Six Forces. Every Force that we have needs improvement through our dreams in equal measure. Admittedly, that can vary over time—depending on how our life's going. But each Force needs our attention.

All of the foregoing I wanted to mention: lest you assume that the dream work I'm teaching you comes with academic degrees or peer review. It's simply me-- after all my years of down-to-earth, day-after-day searching for the good in dreams.

...Okay, now, let us get back to the second dream and what value it has for me.

What's my experience with last night's second dream? (We are on The Sexual Force.))

Without a lot of thought: my past-recall is that my mother was less than helpful in my adolescent development of sex. It's just a sense I have that she herself was not savvy in what to tell a boy. So when she shows up in this dream— with questions about my new activities—which have to do with new-found romance with my fifty years' wife-- my rejection of Mom is a sign I'm on the right path.

When a dream has someone questioning what I am doing, I tend to be cautious. It's quite possible she is there to advise me and steer me to a better path.

But in this instance I recall how Mom was… and doubt her wisdom for my guidance. People can be there to serve as well as not to…

How does this dream help to improve the Force I'm working on?

When behavior-changes occur in life, dreams often come to reinforce their worth. Such reinforcement gives us confidence that what we are doing is the right thing. The fact that what we are doing is not even mentioned in the dream means that we have to identify it outside of the dream. Perhaps it's just the dream's way of getting us to bring to the dream our own recollection.

Part of growing our life is being willing to do some of the work on our own.

You will find as you get older, that part of the thrill of "being" is coming up with some of the answers, yourself… There is nothing like that feeling when you're learning.

...

Would you agree that the presence of long trousers in this dream may point to a more mature way of living (and maybe "wearing the pants" in a fresh relationship with one's longtime spouse)? Doesn't seeing meaning like that improve this Force I'm on?

...And doesn't the scene of a green blanket being covered over the bed give you a sense: that the question of what's right in a marriage is being put to rest and answered with true finality?

These are the sorts of dream pictures you, too, will have and be able to understand-- as you ask yourself how the dream helps improve the Force you are on. It's worth your while.

YOUR GOALS: TO BE SMOKE-FREE AND STRIVE TO BE THRIVING

DAY#24—WEDNESDAY—THE MOVING FORCE

IMPROVE YOUR MOVING FORCE THROUGH DREAMS—TO ACHIEVE YOUR GOALS!

WRITTEN UP DREAMS	*JOTTED DOWN DREAMS*

DAILY QUESTIONS TO ASK EACH OF THE DREAMS YOU HAVE:

#1.) WHAT'S MY EXPERIENCE WITH THIS DREAM FROM LAST NIGHT?

#2.) HOW DOES THIS DREAM IMPROVE THE FORCE I'M WORKING ON?

DAY TWENTY-FOUR—WEDNESDAY—THE MOVING FORCE

One act I would warn you against now is the act of "pushing" too hard with dreams. This is a fault I find myself committing when I become most intensified in having supportive dreams… and I push too hard.

The instance I try to force dreams to do my own bidding, that's often the instance when there is a disconnect in my getting assistance from my dreams for my goal.

Often, rather than helping me with my particular goal to improve my Force-- dreams demean me with dreams of my impatient zest to wring the right stuff dreams can give. I sense that is just what happened last night with the two dreams I found myself having.

Here is the first dream to show you:

*   *   *   *

Dream #1:'Two old friends are horsing around. One fellow keeps on bothering the other till the other guy has had enough and gets hold of him and messes up his hair and smacks his face around. I stand there witnessing it all and feeling badly that the one getting beaten up couldn't foresee how the other was on the verge of his having enough of his taunting at some point. Most would have ended it long ago.'

What's my experience with this first dream last night?

As I witnessed this goings-on, I couldn't help but think, 'What a waste it all was. It shouldn't have happened at all.'

Both of these guys were grown. They should each have respect for the other. After all, they had grown up together. They should have known better.

It reminded me of just how my behavior was in the act of bugging my patient dream source. Then finally my dream source had enough and took after my poor behavior. The result was a frustrated knockabout. Nothing was accomplished.

As far as how this dream improved the Force I'm working on: about all it improved was to show me (once more) I can't push, push, push to receive dreams that improve that Force --The Moving Force.

So how can I avoid this sort of thing from ever happening? If I try to relax as I prepare myself for sleep that ought to help matters.

Most of us think that if we push the "buttons in life" that bring us our benefits, we are better off than if we just submissively wait for benefits to come. In the case of dreams, we are better off if we relax with the understanding that dreams know what we need...After all, they are part of us. As long as we express trust and faith in the role dreams play, they should honor us with the right message we need.

Here is the next dream to show you:

*   *   *   *

Dream #2: 'I open up a large cabinet and take out a cereal plate. On it I see a small bug crawling. I bring it into the kitchen and show my wife. The bug falls off the plate onto the linoleum floor. Just before, a friend of mine had said he'd read a book of mine and hesitated to tell me how he found it. I acted as if his own opinion was no big deal--whether it was good or bad.'

What's my experience with last night's second dream?

Although you would think there's nothing wrong with opening up a large cabinet and taking out a cereal plate, the way this dream came off: I felt as if I was prying into something that I shouldn't be... Plus finding a bug in this process made me react negatively.

Coupling that with the friend hesitating to tell me what he thought about my book left me with feeling these events were bugging me.

What's much better for a writer than to welcome what a reader thinks of his book?

There are tons of book published each day...That someone

would take the time to read mine is a compliment-- even if he found the book unpleasant.

From the way the guy had said (he "wasn't sure what to say"), I formed the impression he wasn't pleased with me…Nevertheless, I should hear him.

If we're asking for those truths that dreams proffer us, we should welcome all of the truths— regardless whether they strike us as good or bad.

How does this dream improve the Force I am now working on?

Again, I must relax and be ready for what dreams say. I ought always rejoice that I am actually making contact with this great source. It is like finding a revered guide on the top of a mountain and taking in whatever he tells me. The wisdom found in dreams is far greater than any that I generally have.

If we looked deep enough, I believe we would find that all of human progress and human understanding first arrives in somebody's mind-- through the gift of one's dreams—whether one's aware of this source or has no sense of it.

As a human being you're just as much in line to benefit as anyone.

YOUR GOALS: TO BE SMOKE-FREE AND STRIVE TO BE THRIVING

DAY#25—THURSDAY—THE FEELING FORCE

IMPROVE YOUR FEELING FORCE THROUGH DREAMS—TO ACHIEVE YOUR GOALS!

WRITTEN UP DREAMS	*JOTTED DOWN DREAMS*

DAILY QUESTIONS TO ASK EACH OF THE DREAMS YOU HAVE:

#1.) WHAT'S MY EXPERIENCE WITH THIS DREAM FROM LAST NIGHT?

#2.) HOW DOES THIS DREAM IMPROVE THE FORCE I'M WORKING ON?

DAY TWENTY-FIVE—THURSDAY—THE FEELING FORCE

This first dream—I think—is closely akin to what a lot of folks experience— leaving them with a sense of liberation or fulfillment. Once we've perused this dream, let's look more at this common experience.

So here's the first dream that I had:

* * * *

Dream #1: 'This was a very strange liberating dream. It mentioned "feeling" numerous times. I experienced a flow of sensations that left me certain and confident that I was moving in the right direction. The funny thing was I made no move to write anything down. When I woke up—it was if I had been on a sort of review without much desire to record it. (Something seldom experienced.)

What's my experience with this first dream last night?

I can only report my sense of experiencing waves of exuberance. It was as if a change occurred in a part of my self that I couldn't pinpoint.

Was there something in me better than it had been before? If so, what brought that on? I couldn't say. And I hadn't written down anything. There was not even a wish to do that.

Usually when I wake up, I try to grab a pen and write down whatever I can remember. But in this case I had no energy for that.

So how did this dream help improve the Force I'm working on?

I cannot really say. But within me, I felt better. And this is the sort of feeling I think folks get from special dreams.

The process starts with all manner of folks delaying decisions. (That isn't done so consciously.)

A person is faced with a major decision that could be life-changing for him. Without thinking about what his "retreat-delay" means, he says to the other one (who's waiting to hear what his decision will be): "Look... before I decide on

this, I'd like to sleep on it." And that is what he tries.
The next morning he awakens and prepares for the day.

Has anything happened during his sleep that has given him any direction to make that decision? He may, indeed, have had a dream, which he has remembered; and it clearly advised him not to go ahead with what the other guy wanted him to agree to. The dream might have been quite explicit in warning him against it. But more than likely: what really happened was that he woke up with absolutely no recollection of a dream-- but with a discovered sense of the decision that he ought to make now.

In other words, the dream he had would have been forgotten, but the effect of it lingered with him; and he now feels that he should or shouldn't choose what he's asked to do.

Folks have used the "retreat" for years. Haven't you, yourself, heard of people using it? If not, ask your parents-- or folks who are older than you. I think you'll find that they know the "retreat" and maybe have even used it, themselves.

The irony is that most people have no idea why the "retreat's" used....It's become an expression that folks use when they're in the dark about which way to go--when they simply aren't sure. Folks have learned to delay their choice at that very moment.

Of course, the next day, they may have had a dream that left them with a sense of closure— which they don't remember— but at least they have decided in favor of or not in favor of something. Either way, they can decide now.

There are instances, too, when folks wake to a new idea that solves some question. They don't remember what they dreamed, but in it an idea was hatched to help them.

(Poor dreams! They often do not get any credit for all the great gifts they grant folks.)

Hopefully now you will begin to comprehend how dreams can help guide you in life.

And maybe as you work with me in this program you will have

a dream you may not recall, but it will tell you how devastating it would be for you even to smoke one quick cigarette. And that is well and good.

It's happened to me that something I'm scarcely pondering on somehow produces a new insight— mainly because I experienced a dream that dealt with that thing.

And certainly from the dream that I have just described, my Feeling Force seems stronger.

...Let's look at the next dream last night
*   *   *   *.

Dream #2: 'I happen to have a conversation with my manager in which he states we need certain oil tanks and oil to satisfy some federal or state requirements. While he was talking, this guy was driving his car. One of my truck drivers had just told me he was going over to pick up some of the stated requirements now. But I asked this fellow, my manager, 'Don't we already have the tanks and oil?' (It seemed to me that we already had them both.) He hesitates and started to explain that what we have may not pass inspection. (But I wasn't sure that was so.)'

What's my experience with last night's second dream?

I have to share with you a fault that I've had that concerns my impatient feelings. So many times in business people have told me that I should go ahead and do something, and then much later I find out that they were mistaken or acting out of careless authority.

When I was faced with folks' sorry advisories, I would always get impatient with the perception of having to check what they were telling me... I didn't want to waste time researching the question and making sure they were right.

Now in this dream I'm being informed by my manager... yet here I am not in such a hurry to do what he's saying. I'm willing to delay the decision to buy more stuff. If I have to, it seems I will make darned certain that I don't spend money on what I really do not need.

My hesitancy's a big improvement to the Force I'm currently

working on. It reveals a new sense: that even if I don't much care to dig into the wordage of the new requirements, I am through with going ahead from someone else's words—until I determine the answer that satisfies me.

Have you, yourself, suffered the same conflict I've had: people tell you stuff, and you are unwilling to see for yourself if they are right.

Perhaps you'll have a dream like mine.

The point is: this dream gives me the energy and insight to see what my fault was and to inculcate an expanse of confidence that forces me to check things out before I take someone else's advice on it.

Can you see how dreams can help you (in just this one instance) save yourself a lot of grief and expense that needn't be?

My own advice from dreams has been that the crucial most important word that's in the English language is "No". (We hear things that we are asked to do, and mostly "No" is the answer we need to respond with—at least till we prove to our satisfaction that "Yes" is the answer.)

You may not agree, but my advice is: check stuff yourself.

YOUR GOALS: TO BE SMOKE-FREE AND STRIVE TO BE THRIVING

DAY#26—FRIDAY—THE THINKING FORCE

IMPROVE YOUR THINKING FORCE THROUGH DREAMS—TO ACHIEVE YOUR GOALS!

WRITTEN UP DREAMS	*JOTTED DOWN DREAMS*

DAILY QUESTIONS TO ASK EACH OF THE DREAMS YOU HAVE:

#1.) WHAT'S MY EXPERIENCE WITH THIS DREAM FROM LAST NIGHT?

#2.) HOW DOES THIS DREAM IMPROVE THE FORCE I'M WORKING ON?

DAY TWENTY-SIX—FRIDAY—THE THINKING FORCE:
* * * *

Dream #1: 'The man gave a nice speech. His microphone was on the underside of the framing that the man stood under. (There was something about "underside" that made me wonder.)'

What's my experience with this first dream last night?

I didn't care much for his speech— even though-- as I dreamed—it was a nice speech. The word that concerned me was "underside". That's a word that connotes something that's not so good— something that we don't' want to see.

It's revealing how a dream shows us its meaning with some simple innuendo that casts the dream in a very different light.

If "underside" weren't in the dream, there wouldn't be much there. There would be no viewpoint.

So when you dream, pay attention to what key word you dream that may help you discern what the dream was hoping you'd see.

…Soon you may realize: the composition of the dream reveals an insightful guide that's in back of it. That in itself should fill you with surprise and amazement. To think that billions of folks live out their lives with scant or no thought to what dreams say, strikes me as a neglect of immense proportions.

So having said how I witnessed the above mentioned dream, let me ask myself, 'How does the dream help improve the Force I am now working on?'

I need to recognize that-- even if I'd like to think the noblest of thoughts in my day-to-day living— as a human being and with not much sainthood in sight-- I have to accept—as part of the whole-- that I will share with the rest of mankind—deliberations that do not allow me too much pride.

I may be able to give a nice speech, but that doesn't mean

that underneath it there does not lurk aspects of myself that aren't nice.

And I may find myself thinking that I wouldn't want folks (or at least folks I know) to be aware of much of that. Now I could flail myself earnestly when such thoughts come to my mind-- as I've heard tell some saintly folks have done — or I could smile at them and think, 'Big deal! We're all human!' Perhaps robustness is healthier than remorse.

A thriving life allows us all to accept our frail thoughts but dare not follow them.

…Here is the next dream that I had:
    *   *   *   *

Dream #2: 'I'm standing in a line cashing a weekly check. I forget that all deductions have already been made and ask the guy taking care of people to deduct some amounts, which confuses him. While he's struggling to see how to make the deductions, I realize he does not need to bother with them. Someone says that Tom Cruise is going to be tired of waiting his turn—with all the delay that is being caused.'

What's my experience with last night's second dream?

The reason why it's important to start off with saying what our experience is with a dream: is because in doing so we don't have to bother with "meaning" or how the dream helps improve us.

Getting caught up--at first-- in a dream's meaning is no way to go. We all make the mistake of asking what something means before we try to discern what it tells us—or what experience we have when we view it.

Viewing this dream I detect I'm being very careless in dealing with the clerk. I have confused him with my lack of remembering to be specific about telling him: 'Don't take deductions.'

I have caused the fellow to waste a lot of time that he could have spent with "Tom Cruise".

So how does this dream help improve my Thinking Force?

What could I have done to avoid the confusion I sowed?

Suppose-- before I came head-to-head with the check cashing guy-- I had rehearsed what I was going to say:

Me: 'I have a check in my hand and want you to cash it.'
That's all I'd have to say. The deductions were made before…
The check was in my hand. So I've nothing to add except,
'Please cash this check for me.'

Now I will concede that inner babbling about what one's going to do before one actually does it sounds quite idiotic; but in this dream --as clearly shown-- I glean I'm to make a "prep-plan" for my actions.

The point is: if I didn't make the mistake of giving the cash check man extra work, I would have made his life a lot simpler that moment. There's something good in that.

When we think of how our day went, wouldn't it be nice to think that we made some guy's life easier by our kindness?

…Here is the third dream that I also dreamed last night. Again, I just wrote it down first:

   *   *   *   *

Dream #3: 'I'm revisiting New Orleans with a friend. We enter a section (in the dream) where the streets are real narrow and the brick walls look as if they're eight to ten feet tall. Apparently it's some sort of break time—in that no one is walking around—until a few minutes have elapsed. We have set our bikes against a doorway and dicker about safety in our leaving them there. It seemed foolish to risk such theft.'

What's my experience with this third dream last night? (That is the first question you ask after you've written up your dream from the jot-down that you've made once you've awakened):

I was amazed the way New Orleans was in one area where the narrow streets and tall walls were seen. I've never glimpsed walls that were quite that tall. And why were they?

…Then the sudden influx of pedestrians out of nowhere gave me a startle.

…Now indecision reigned about whether to leave our bikes in somebody's doorway.

So: how does this dream help improve the Force that I'm working on now?

A mentor once told me: whenever I start to worry about whether I should do anything, the best course of action is: decide on it then. In other words, don't put off what should be decided now— the primary reason being that it's one's Thinking Force advising us to steer ourselves clear of danger.

If we don't deal with our worry-- when it runs through our minds-- we'll later regret it.

Leaning a bike against someone's doorway--in this day's a guarantee for its theft. I and my friend sensed that, yet we gambled danger instead of securing safety.

Now I'm going to risk a guess here that might amuse you —as seemingly far-fetched-----yet maybe "New Orleans" lives in the dream to warn me and propose to me that I form a "New Our-Leans" mindset that I never leave stuff unless sure of safety.

Maybe the high walls and narrow streets are to instill in me the new policy—It's high and It's narrow—that I won't ever forget it-- instilling in me to make this dream one I'll remember and one that helps me to improve my Thinking Force.

…Here's the last dream I had last night:

*   *   *   *

Dream #4:'There was a dream where a question came up: who should be the guide for a group I'm in? I knew both candidates from the days we were in a tennis group together. (That didn't enter into the dream.) I was about ready to stand up and speak on behalf of one of them. I thought he was much more insightful and intelligent and more able to speak in an optimistic way. The room was filled with people belonging to this group, and a number of them stood to speak on someone's behalf.'

What's my experience with this fourth dream last night?

I liked both of these fellows, and I wasn't real happy to nominate one of them over the other. I don't like picking sides in front of both of the prospects. And maybe I didn't have to... Maybe other folks would cause the vote to be held without my voice entering in. And when the vote came, I would just abstain from it.

But the dream forced me to take sides-- if only in the sense I'd aid my favorite.

So then, how would this dream improve my Thinking Force?

Anytime we can verbalize whatever it is that we are faced with choosing --the more thriving becomes our life. A life without speaking or thinking words is a life that is lost to ignorance.

… And if we don't learn to say out loud to others or inwardly to our own selves, "Smoking is the dumbest thing anyone can do!" then we risk our arriving at the den of smokers where words are never spoken.

So often we all find ourselves doing things that we have never verbalized on. That's dangerous and un-thriving.

YOUR GOALS: TO BE SMOKE-FREE AND STRIVE TO BE THRIVING

DAY#27—SATURDAY—THE HIGHER FEELING FORCE

IMPROVE YOUR HIGHER FEELING FORCE THROUGH DREAMS—TO ACHIEVE YOUR GOALS!

WRITTEN UP DREAMS	JOTTED DOWN DREAMS

DAILY QUESTIONS TO ASK EACH OF THE DREAMS YOU HAVE:

#1.) WHAT'S MY EXPERIENCE WITH THIS DREAM FROM LAST NIGHT?

#2.) HOW DOES THIS DREAM IMPROVE THE FORCE I'M WORKING ON?

DAY TWENTY-SEVEN—SATURDAY—THE HIGHER FEELING FORCE

How are you feeling with your new dream work these days? Are you getting guidance out of the dreams that I show you? Are the dreams I show you giving you a sense of how to go about working with your own personal dreams? That's the purpose of my sharing.

If you're just reading my dreams without doing yours, then both of us have failed the task. Here is what our task is: My task is to show you clearly how to work with your dreams. If that hasn't been clear, then I have failed my task. Your task: is to take what I have shown you with my own dreams and use them for your own... Every step I take can be yours.

Why are we doing this? For one immense reason: Dreams help us to learn for ourselves. In dreams our Unconscious teaches us how to live free from smoking and how to live a life that is thriving.

Do you know anyone who can teach you in a way that improves all your Forces and guides you to achieve the goals that we have here set forth? I don't think there's a soul who can do that for you.

All the teachers who are around may teach you what they have found to be true in life (whether how to keep from smoking or how to live their lives in a thriving manner). But messages from their lifestyle won't necessarily translate to your lifestyle.

What we all need are messages that come from within us. We must find that input. Teachers' inputs are not enough. I won't say to avoid respectable teachers. But with them you only listen. Your input is quite small. Listening doesn't cut it.

With the method I here propose, you are the one who asks your dreams to convince you that smoking is not what you need. Certain dreams will come to you and--with your resolve-- create a scene in some manner that will influence you never to start smoking.

How can that be?. "How can my dreams" (You may ask)

"keep me from ever starting to smoke? Isn't this some vein of voodoo?"

(No, it's not.) Within us there is an Unconscious that Nature has placed there at the very beginning of our existence on Earth. At one time, it may have been our Unconscious that ruled our lives more than our Conscious.

Our Unconscious has more knowledge— more wisdom than we know— and by our acquainting ourselves with it –through our dream work-- we will begin to reap the benefits it shares. (Follow me more with this reasoning.)

Since smoking is such an affront to our nature my hope is you will be able to learn from your dream work-- thanks to your Unconscious— the smoking-truth. The side bonus is that you will also --through your dream work—begin to live a life that is thriving. Maybe you already live a life close to that— yet all of us can learn much more how to live such a life by writing down our dreams and learning how to apply them.

Once you start writing down your dreams every night and early in the morning—as hopefully you are now— new ideas and thoughts-- and much, much more--will come to you.

…Let me continue to share what my dreams have been and how some worth has come from them:

*   *   *   *

Dream #1:'Rush Limbaugh is talking about two pipes that are in Canada that exist next to each other…The next thing I know I am in Canada with a large body of water on my right; and there is Rush Limbaugh climbing high up on a ladder next to the pipes. He climbs probably a hundred feet—I hardly could make out his form. He is conversing with someone as he stands at the highest point. Now he starts climbing down. Then he gets to a point where he has to swim in some water that flows in. He splashes across the short distance in his street clothes and then continues his climb down. I'm so impressed with his dedication to a first-hand understanding of the situation he spoke of. I'd like to go up to him and shake his hand.'

What's my experience with this first dream last night?

Well-- in the dream-- I pretty much appreciate all that Rush Limbaugh has done there.

What has he done? (Weird as it was) He went directly to the source of facts he had been telling folks-- just to see what he'd been talking about.

How does this dream improve the Force that I am working on?

Rush showed a great trait—and one I am slowly in the process of inculcating: When I hear fresh talk or read new thoughts, I try to check all out on the Internet and achieve a better understanding therewith.

Of course, what Rush did was beyond any normal pursuit; but exaggeration often makes the point more sharply than someone's calm advice.

And here's something that's fun--when you're working on a dream's gist: Just look at Rush Limbaugh's name and how it might mean something that helps us improve more:

We all know what Rush means: He is in a hurry. His first name is easy to grasp. But any idea what his last name might mean? Often with names it's more the sound of it that gives the clue-- rather than the spelling. Limbaugh sounds just like "limbo" sounds. And "limbo" is a state of uncertainty or not knowing what is going on. So here he is "rushing to get to the source of uncertainty." Rush spoke about the Canadian pipes, which he knew little of. So off he trots to have a look and to add much more to his life experience.

Now as I said, who would do that? But it helps us to see the point the dream's making: It's good to learn more about things.

Plus if we start to do something we think is right and dreams come and reinforce it: that helps us to perceive that we're on the right track.

...Let's take the next dream that I had:

  *   *   *   *

Dream #2: 'I am sitting in my home office-study when my Mother comes in with many notes from various folks who have called me. The notes were in a thick packet, and I just skimmed through them for a moment. There was also a note from a guy who (in the dream) delivers papers to me every day. His note revealed he was also in some promotion and had written something I could scarcely read—though it seemed to say if I'd done something and it didn't work—it's time to forget it...Later I'm in a car with someone who had last been seen in a Mercedes convertible. She had driven it on a trial basis and then turned it in. I asked how she liked it. She replied that it was okay. I said, 'I imagine you have always wanted to drive one—then you drive it. And you find it's fine but not as great as you thought.' I then said, 'It's like trying on a thousand dollar suit. It feels great, but so what?' At that point we stopped in front of a deli—which has been in our neighborhood.'

(You may get tired of this) but the first question is: what has been my experience as I looked at this dream? What did I get from it?

For a long time I longed for the fast life... the life with cars and the life with rich clothes. I'm older, but it just might be that deep down I still might like to afford such things. But somewhere else within myself I recognize that so much of that longing is blown out of sight. We are hustled by promotion people to make ourselves richer-- either looking or rich in fact.

My experience with this dream warns otherwise. The deli is closer to me (where things are down-to-earth and nothing's outrageous.)

Now to turn to our next question: How does this dream improve the Force I'm working on?

For myself, I am better not longing for Mercedes or thousand dollar suits. They're so hyped up for what they are.

Yet now I'll emphasize: This dream is meant for me, and it just might not be for you. I show it to you as an example of how I can learn more about myself and what works for me. Would you say that's worth knowing ?

How many of us have gotten our values from within? How many of us have been told what we should strive after— without our being in a position to say what we believe is right for us? Dreams are a way for us to learn what's right for us.

Let's look at the next and last dream:

*　　　　　*　　　　　*　　　　　*

Dream #3: 'An employee of mine (in the dream) and I go across the street where two large steel figures are standing. On the necks of these statues were thick strands of multi-colored Mardi Gras beads. There may have also been a cross sticking out from each figure there. Apparently a third figure had already been sold. We looked at these figures with a wholesome awe. I wasn't sure if my steel firm had made them or we bought them.'

What's my experience with this third dream last night?

Before I go over this dream, I want to mention that it's important for me to try as hard as possible to write about dreams as soon as they happen. If I wait past the next day or further, I seem to feel more of a detachment from the dream than when I review it the immediate day after I've dreamed it.

If I fail, I know what happens. Intervening life takes me further away from the dream-- which can lessen impact.

In this third dream I was unable to work with it right after I had dreamed it. I was delayed. Let's see what my experience is with work one day afterwards:

Reviewing these statues I sense they have a calm and reverent sense about them. I have to say: 'They seemed almost hallowed to me.' They stand there in total darkness. The beads reminded me of the beads people wear at Mardi Gras celebrations. But the crosses coaxed in me solemnness that caused me to be still.

Often in dreams we may find a motif that is different from what we're used to in our own Faith. I'm of the Jewish Faith

— while the Cross is Christian. Some folks might turn away from that— they may fear this dreaming of symbols that won't fit with their own faith.

I have found that these new influences ought never to be shunned. They allow me to broaden my life and be more thriving. Just because I have been born into one Faith doesn't mean I cannot take on the values of other Faiths.

…So here I am—faced with colored beads and crosses. Isn't there a fuller freedom, which is being offered to me? It's not that freedom that proclaims "Anything Goes!" But more of a freedom that grants me a new acceptance for what others might know.

How does this dream improve the Force that I am working on?

Be open to others' ways of dealing with life and death--with celebrations of the holy and profane.

I may be a bit guilty of "stretching" this dream to help me to improve my life, but the effort I have made may make a dent upon my Higher Thinking Force now.

I believe that whatever we come up with—following the effort we've made—gives us a result to be proud of.

Try to muster up the courage and commitment to deal with dreams as I have shown.

YOUR GOALS: TO BE SMOKE-FREE AND STRIVE TO BE THRIVING

DAY#28—SUNDAY—THE HIGHER THINKING FORCE

IMPROVE YOUR HIGHER THINKING FORCE THROUGH DREAMS—TO ACHIEVE YOUR GOALS!

WRITTEN UP DREAMS	*JOTTED DOWN DREAMS*

DAILY QUESTIONS TO ASK EACH OF THE DREAMS YOU HAVE:

#1.) WHAT'S MY EXPERIENCE WITH THIS DREAM FROM LAST NIGHT?

#2.) HOW DOES THIS DREAM IMPROVE THE FORCE I'M WORKING ON?

DAY TWENTY-EIGHT—SUNDAY—THE HIGHER THINKING FORCE

You may have already asked yourself-- or started to ask yourself: "Just because I dream something that you say improves one Force, how does that Force translate its improvement into the wholeness of my life? "

And the answer is: usually that one dream won't necessarily cause a change in all of you. But it's a start.

And yet, there are dreams that improve one Force so powerfully they do impose change on the others.

But most of the time: a dream--improving one Force—starts building a foundation for improving more Forces... until at some point you find yourself in the act of change.

I will warn you that if you were to ask yourself, "How'd change happen?" ...You may not know. Sometimes change is subtle; all you can think is, 'I've changed because of combinations in dreams that have brought me to where I really feel comfortable thriving in life in ways I never knew... And as far as smoking: there's no way I could begin that.'

...Here is a dream that I had last night—for this day that's devoted to my Higher Thinking Force. Let's look at it for a moment and then see what's my experience.

*   *   *   *

Dream #1:'I look over a huge acreage that hasn't been developed yet and picture how many buildings could be built on it Then I work with a large crane operator parceling off the new development. I see another pair of men working on another site that is adjacent to mine. I survey one area that's already covered with buildings constructed in the last few years. They inspire me.'

What's my experience with this first dream last night?

I hope you can sense how much I must have been inspired by seeing those buildings-- which already were built—that made me think how I could make the plain ground I stood on look much like that developed site. It was a terrific spectacle, and I felt excited as I started work.

How does this dream improve the Force I'm working on?

This dream is a strong metaphor for how you and I can build our own buildings on the open plots of acreage we all have that exist in our Higher Thinking Force. We need to remember: that everyone who has done anything in his life (that helps us) started with a bare plot of land (within) and somehow figured out how to build what he then believed.

Every one of us tends to believe that the "do-gooder" had it easier— but the chances are: he may have had it harder.

This is the sort of dream that we should try to keep in mind as we begin to live without smoking and thrivingly.

You don't build the kind of buildings we're talking of and start smoking. Those two won't mix. If you are a "builder" —you can't be a smoker. You can't live to thrive and still smoke.

…I had a second dream last night that went like this:(We'll discuss it once you've read it.)

*   *   *   *

Dream #2:'A group of us become interested in an artist who paints and plan on him producing a few works of art every year and buying them accordingly.'

What's my experience with last night's second dream?

I awakened with a mean thought— as a group of us were going to secure some guy's output in order to make much money from his work. I guess patrons plan that; and maybe there's nothing wrong there. But it struck me that our controlling someone's work almost makes him a slave to us.

On the other hand, an artist can suffer want-- living off of what his means are. So this group would finance his life's independence. He would not starve and could focus simply on his art work.

Some dreams show us doing what we really ought not to do. And I felt this dream was more or less showing that.

So how did the dream help improve the Force I'm working on?

Rather than control the artist-- who was only dreamed of— I should focus on my own abilities and give them the time they need to thrive.

So often we shortchange ourselves by neglecting to grant ourselves time for thriving on some talent or gift that we have discovered (through our dream work) that we possess.

We can't go off to the woods and concentrate on say one talent— but we can find a way to work with it as we comply with the obligations we bear in life.

This may be a good time to emphasize that the dream work we are talking about should never hurt the folks who are part of our lives.

It's possible that we find out from our dreams that certain folks are not good for us. They may be friends we've had for years who are leading us off in directions that our dreams indicate are bad for us.

Common sense may have told us such-- had we listened— but here we are: faced with the choice of sticking with "friends" and ending up with problems or figuring out a way that we can-- without hurting them—finish the friendship.

In any case, never act with superiority or cockiness –when you take steps to do what you have to.

There's a danger: we think just because we have some connection with our Unconscious and have greater insights than our friends may have, that we can act as if they don't count. Everyone has his life; yet our goal is to keep from smoking and live thrivingly.

Our goal is not to set friends straight about our truths. Our truths may not be theirs. Yet, our primary duty is to focus on our life— and not to set other folks straight.

Of course, if a dream speaks of our need to talk with others about some matter... fine.

But let us not make the mistake that others have often made: that once they've learned what makes their world go 'round, they want to convince others of their new truths and fresh findings.

Often the wisest course is the one that ruffles the least feathers and gives one peace.

YOUR GOALS: TO BE SMOKE-FREE AND STRIVE TO BE THRIVING

DAY#29—MONDAY—THE INSTINCTIVE FORCE

IMPROVE YOUR INSTINCTIVE FORCE THROUGH DREAMS—TO ACHIEVE YOUR GOALS!

WRITTEN UP DREAMS	*JOTTED DOWN DREAMS*

DAILY QUESTIONS TO ASK EACH OF THE DREAMS YOU HAVE:

#1.) WHAT'S MY EXPERIENCE WITH THIS DREAM FROM LAST NIGHT?

#2.) HOW DOES THIS DREAM IMPROVE THE FORCE I'M WORKING ON?

DAY TWENTY-NINE—MONDAY—THE INSTINCTIVE FORCE

Here is the first dream that I struggled with last night. I'd like to share it with you now:

* * * *.

Dream #1: 'Something concerning the multiplying of five million people times two million people that adds up to the unbelievable amount of ten billion people.'

What's my experience with this first dream last night?

In this dream, I am struggling with how such numbers compute. Here's two million people—and there are five million people…

How does one work through the multiplication of both of those groups. I was perplexed. Even while I'm dreaming I am wondering what the word 'times' means in mathematics.

It's simpler to picture adding and subtracting and dividing. But how does one multiply ('times') people?

When I awoke, I wrote down the dream but was just as stumped…I figured you can't use mathematics to 'times' people. You can add and subtract but can never 'times them'

So how does this dream help to improve the Force I am on? (It's the Instinctive Force.)

This dream obliquely gets me to think: 'folks can't be reduced to quantities you can multiply together. Their spirit just won't let that be.'

…Learning instinctively draws me closer to the earth and to new reality that's far from unconcern and close to a belief in concepts of human worth.

…The next two dreams are a tad on the trashy side. We can learn from them just as well.

Scatological dreams—you may be surprised—have as much

worth as high-minded stuff.

It would be easy to turn away from crude dreams, but from my point of view, we need to deal with them, so that we can Improve all our base and complex humanity

Even vulgar dreams have a purpose to help us improve—although often it's hard to tell what that might be. But like comedians who dish out all sorts of coarse things—which tickle us greatly—dreams force embarrassment in our minds and stir us to think.

So with your indulgence I will report what my dreams centered on with this past night:

    *   *   *   *

Dream #2: 'A toilet flushes, but one turd remains on the ledge of the bowl—an event that seems impossible in that the ledge Is level with the topmost point of water…unless overflowing water would bring the turd right up to the ledge and leave it. THE TURD THAT WOULDN'T FLUSH was the title I gave this dream In a jocular vein.'

What's my experience with last night's second dream?

I found myself swiveling my head as I experienced this dream. The fact that I'm writing this book to help ninth grade readers learn how to keep themselves from smoking—as well as to live a thriving life—leaves me with the question: 'why write down this garbage?'

Yet probably some—if not all—ninth graders will have crude dreams and want to dump them. Please note that one ought never to be scornful of such dreams—as long as you observe our two questions.

The first: 'what's your own dream experience?' And the second to ask, 'How does this dream improve the Force you are now working on?'

So let us—or let me—ask, 'How does this dream improve the Force I am working on?' The key task is to work with the title I've given it.

    THE TURD THAT WOULDN'T FLUSH jocularly states that even

with turds there are those that simply won't flush away. And though no one wants to be termed a 'turd', the dream stresses what we should remember: as we work on our lives and concentrate on thriving, we should not let ourselves be easily flushed away.

If this turd won't flush, how much more resistance should we give the constraints that want us to give up on our goals in life?

Here's another dream that tests our broadmindedness—as well as self-criticism.

*   *   *   *

Dream #3: 'I am at my steel firm—dressed a bit fancier than usual. I walk down to an apartment building in a neighborhood that's not where the firm actually is (in real life). I enter a rest room and notice a problem in the toilet. I use a plunger till the waste has been engulfed. I then try to go myself…I notice our steel truck as it pulls out of the street—only loaded with a few stops. Someone asks me to call on my phone to see if this small load should be delivered. I personally thought that maybe it should be. I'm told, "Not yet." Rather than sit on the john, I grab hold of a high window sill and hang from there with my butt arched over the toilet bowl and defecate like that. Also in this dream a wagon is rolling down a hill on a parking lot of the neighborhood super market.'

What's my experience with this third dream last night?

It wasn't a picnic for me. I sensed I was being sucker-punched in my gut. I'm struck with all the points that are being made in this dream.

First, I'm dressed fancier…Then I'm in a filthy rest room. I'm experiencing that place as super-gross.

I am also a 'message-boy'—asking about whether to send a truck out now. I always felt that it made sense to deliver what's done even if some orders that were promised were not ready. But the head of shipping had other ideas and overruled what I wanted.

It didn't seem that I was very much in charge.

So how in the world does this dream improve the Force I am currently working on?

Am I the boss I think I am? Am I proud of what I am doing in this dream? I would say, 'No…I'm wasting time. I'm concerned about dress, but not about business or guiding others to constantly pursue it.'

Can you picture a fancily dressed dude engaged in what I found myself doing? There's a saying that describes the scene depicted here: "He's flapping his wings in vain!"

Even at the lowest level of my being, I should always keep in mind what my job is. Even though I am now retired from the steel business, the dream iterates that if I'm the boss again, think just what the boss should be.

We gain strength from tweaking weakness.

Do you know the saying, "falling off the wagon"? It refers to a person who ends up doing just what he's not supposed to do. That looks pretty much like me here.

In the dream I need to figure out how to jump on the wagon and change my ways.

…Here's another dream that touches on a weakness: (One that's ingrained is hard to change.)

   *   *   *   *

Dream #4: 'I am standing in some exercise group next to a neighbor of mine with quite a pornographic last name. We are being urged—though I hear no one commanding us—to sort of lean back with our feet firmly planted on the ground. As we do this, a bushy-tailed squirrel comes close to my neighbor, but leaves him and appears next to me—and somehow gets his swishing tail to reach up to my crotch. I stand there transfixed in fear.'

What's my experience with this last dream last night?

I am squeamish with animals that I consider wild. I don't know why that is—although some fears originate from how others around us (in our formative years) have shown how they might react.

So when this squirrel's tail is banging against my crotch, it frightens me unbearably.

So how would such a dream as this help to improve the Force that I am working on? (Still the Instinctive Force)

When I experience what's happening, it's almost as if the squirrel Is being friendly, and I'm the one who's untrusting. It's not like he's nipping at my poor crotch. He is wagging his tail.

I don't know how I could ever be comfortable with a situation like this, but isn't the dream asking—and trying to get—me to let go of my fear?

As I may once have said, 'What a dream tells you to improve (in your Seven Forces) doesn't mean you'll improve it now. But it's something to keep in mind and hope that an improvement might someday occur.

YOUR GOALS: TO BE SMOKE-FREE AND STRIVE TO BE THRIVING

DAY#30—TUESDAY—THE SEXUAL FORCE

IMPROVE YOUR SEXUAL FORCE THROUGH DREAMS—TO ACHIEVE YOUR GOALS!

WRITTEN UP DREAMS	*JOTTED DOWN DREAMS*

DAILY QUESTIONS TO ASK EACH OF THE DREAMS YOU HAVE:

#1.) WHAT'S MY EXPERIENCE WITH THIS DREAM FROM LAST NIGHT?

#2.) HOW DOES THIS DREAM IMPROVE THE FORCE I'M WORKING ON?

DAY THIRTY—TUESDAY—THE SEXUAL FORCE

It's critical to keep in mind that each night's dream should be connected to the Force that is assigned to it that day. In the present case, the Sexual Force is the Force that's assigned to it this day.

So once I've written down the experience I've had with the dream that's before me, I try to see how that dream helps to improve the Sexual Force.

You may wonder how it's possible to mostly succeed in the execution of fitting the dream to the specific Force that one's working on. Let me see if I can show you-- with the execution that I will now attempt.

So here's the first dream to look at:

      *   *   *   *

Dream #1`:'Someone comes by the house (in the dream it is an old house) and buys a number of copies of a book I wrote many years ago. It was called HOW TO STOP SMOKING IN FIFTY DAYS. No one said anything about this guy coming and buying them. I happened to notice a stack of dollar bills and a bunch of saved newspapers—which may have had something to do with them. There seemed to be a note that five books plus another one were sold. But the pile of cash came up to much more than the normal price of the books... Also someone wanted to know my mother's first name, which I said.'

What's my experience with this first dream last night?

Sales of that book disappointed me; and I tried many avenues for selling it. That may not have been the right book for me to write, inasmuch as I really felt imposed to write a book to keep people FROM SMOKING— not get them TO STOP it.

It happens... once folks start smoking: it's very difficult for them to stop for good. Yes, they may strive to do all sorts of things to stop smoking-- and for a while they'll stop— but sooner or later--for most "ex-smokers"—they'll test their will with one cigarette.

Once they've inhaled that one, they're off to the nearest smoke shop to purchase a full pack. That's why I want earnestly for ninth graders never to start...

... (Now: the dream)... When I learned some fellow had bought six books, I was quite elated; yet at the same time, quite mystified with how it happened. And the fact that no one even said anything when it happened puzzled me more.

Finding all the dollar bills and old newspapers only increased the mystery. There was so much more cash than there really should be.

But the thing that troubled me most was when a guy asked what my mother's first name was. As I told him, it dawned on me: in one part of her name, the sound "dread" could be sensed.

Going further with her first name: the prefix-part of that name could be sounded with a disputing doubt: 'Am I ill.'

Names have a weird way of giving a dreamer clues that he might least be expecting.

How does this dream improve the Force I'm working on?

There's big conflict here: I was glad that someone had bought some of my old books, but "dread" put the kibosh on my gladness.

Could it be that with that book I was uncertain and fearful how folks would take it: an undercurrent of dread that opened up a long lost sense of sexual dread.

With my new book that I'm now building upon, I feel certain there will be no dread.

And the sexual dread— now being brought to light— is simply shown to be silly: an uninformed response from a caring mother, which set up a false barrier that's stayed with me so long without me knowing it...but which I am now free to shed.

Can you see how this dream did its part helping me?

There's nothing I thought I would like better than selling the book I worked so hard on. But then "dread" and "ill" entered in— making me realize how that dread was like the dread put there by my mother long ago.

I don't say this in any way to hurt the memory of my mother, because in her way she was a classy, highly regarded and quite attractive woman… but for me, there must have occurred a response she had to something I did, which left me with long lost feelings of dread.

Yet once I realized how needless that dread was I could smile and bid it farewell— or in this case improve my Sexual Force with a healthier regard for it.

So there you have my thoughts about how this dream helped to improve my Sexual Force.

Frankly--at the start of this writing I've just done-- I didn't have the faintest hint about how this dream could (in any shape or form) improve the Force I'm working on. It would have been easy to turn away from the task and just think, 'There is no way this dream has a thing to do with improving my Sexual Force.'

Here's the magic: When we have the courage or determination to recognize that dreams really do produce—like lessons-- things we can learn much from, we are willing to forge ahead.

I know it is daunting— but once you take it on you will begin to reap rewards that will be priceless and bring you far more than you would ever have thought you'd obtain.

And the beauty part is: this skill's built within you.

…Here is the next dream from last night:
   *   *   *   *

Dream #2: 'An old acquaintance wrote a book on etiquette —according to someone I've known.'

What's my experience with last night's second dream?

This dream left me quite curious to really find out if this guy had written some version of what etiquette is. I can't believe he had— since I've known him for years-- and he'd never impressed me as someone who would do that.

So I did some research— at least the best research I could — and I could not find a thing that showed me he had.

I then wondered: the second guy is the one who said he had written such a book. I couldn't find anything there— short of calling him up and asking him point-blank.

There are actions that I will take-- while working on my dreams-- but asking someone to verify a dream isn't one!.

The purpose of a dream is to improve a Force that currently one's working on-- and not to make one look like he's a bit foolish.

So taking care, what can I do-- after experiencing a kind of frustrating pursuit of facts that can't be found?

How can I see if there is any help that would improve the Force I'm working on?

Let's not overlook the "etiquette" that's mentioned. Is this a word that could improve the Force I'm working on?

Is there such a term--that's called Sexual Etiquette—that might improve me somehow?

Well, it's interesting: There are many blogs that I've found --from Internet clicking--that talk about just what the dream implies:

There surely is something called Sexual Etiquette; and a glance through the blogs was enlightening. I share that term with you, because just saying it has a certain forceful- ness that can surely improve this Force common to us all. These blogs are there for everyone.

What I find with dream work is just what I found here: be- ing willing to check out stuff that's mentioned in a dream can enlarge your mind-world as well as the specific Force you are now working on.

Just imagine if each week-- let alone each day-- you learned something useful to you: how much more thriving your life would be as compared to now!

YOUR GOALS: TO BE SMOKE-FREE AND STRIVE TO BE THRIVING

DAY#31—WEDNESDAY—THE MOVING FORCE

IMPROVE YOUR MOVING FORCE THROUGH DREAMS—TO ACHIEVE YOUR GOALS!

WRITTEN UP DREAMS	*JOTTED DOWN DREAMS*

DAILY QUESTIONS TO ASK EACH OF THE DREAMS YOU HAVE:

#1.) WHAT'S MY EXPERIENCE WITH THIS DREAM FROM LAST NIGHT?

#2.) HOW DOES THIS DREAM IMPROVE THE FORCE I'M WORKING ON?

DAY THIRTY-ONE—WEDNESDAY—THE MOVING FORCE
*   *   *   *

Dream #1:'I am dreaming about SHAWSHANK REDEMPTION, the film—which seems to be unnerving.'

Let me comment on this first dream last night and how I am planning on handling it: All I remember is that I was wrestling while I was dreaming. When I awoke, I felt as if I had been fighting the people or the plot or the way it went.

It was very hard for me to get back to sleep. Consequently, I went to my computer and searched what Wikipedia showed.

I have never seen the movie— although I had seen one of the actors being interviewed on a talk program. From there— curiously-- I read about it, but didn't learn much.

Now I went back and spent more time--as I attempted to follow the plot and find more meaning there.

I have never had a dream that fixated me on a movie. Obviously the wise way to follow up on such a dream is to see the full length of the film. Whatever the dream is saying will grant me the chance to grasp—once I've watched the film. Never let a chance go by to watch a dream's film.

…Sometimes a dream tells us something that we cannot check out in a specific way— like the dream two night's past that said an old acquaintance had written an etiquette book. I couldn't confirm he had. But in this dream, there's a specific film to see.

As things stand now, I am not sure how this dream will improve the Force I'm working on. But I'm certain something moving will develop when I witness the actual film.

Since the dream, I have heard folks say that SHAWSHANK REDEMPTION is the best film they've seen— so there must be something to it that will be worth my while.

I reserved the film at the library and should have it within a couple days. Whenever you have a dream that refers you to something that you can obtain from the library, by all means go for it. (A free service)

Let's go to the next dream and see if we get an eventual benefit there:

*   *   *   *

Dream #2: 'I hear of an old girlfriend and rush to see her. But sad to see, she is in an infant's crib—although she is as beautiful as she was before. I speak with her and say encouraging words to her. I also became involved with another girl whom I promise to see shortly after the dinner time when I'm usually at home. Somehow I think I can call my mother and give her an excuse. All in all I am involved up to my neck with these two and wonder how there's a way out.'

What's my experience with last night's second dream?

I was struck by the strangeness there. In real life I haven't seen this crib-bound girl for over sixty years, although at that time she was a slim, athletic, fresh-faced lass with whom I had a passionate teenager-type romance.

Finding her in a crib, of course, was quite a shocking scene. I acted upbeat and said I'd visit again.

How bizarre that she hadn't grown.

The other girl… I can't remember who she was. But here again, I think she was a girlfriend from the past.

In the dream I must have been rather young, since I was still living with my parents.

In my many years I surely have a tendency to get into a jam with the way I schedule things. I live through them, but it always appears as if I have no common sense that way.

So how does this dream help improve the Force I'm working on?

As in earlier dreams, I need to go over in words—silently in my mind-- just what is transpiring. I don't know if others do that, but I recommend it for time-obligations that you may find yourself facing. It may sound a bit daft, but by verbalizing (like a child might do in a crib) just what's happening in your life--as you live it-- you will defend yourself against such excess scheduling.

You'll find yourself saying, 'I promised to see 'her'(1) sometime; and I promised to see 'her'(2) sometime; and I'm due for dinner at another time… How can I do all of this without my hurting anyone or making them wait? My Moving Force needs to behave in a proper way that allows me to thrive more. There can't be much thriving when my schedule's amok.' (Rushing is a lame way to thrive.)

…Seeing that beautiful girl in a crib forced me to realize I'd deserted any growing up (to respect obligations-in-time) …now to be saddened with.

Sometimes a shocking scene is needed to force one to face up to one's shortcomings.

Is it not amazing that the entire world and all of its experience can be available to you in dreams-- in order to help you improve all your Forces? Is this not but a sheer blessing?

YOUR GOALS: TO BE SMOKE-FREE AND STRIVE TO BE THRIVING

DAY#32—THURSDAY—THE FEELING FORCE

IMPROVE YOUR FEELING FORCE THROUGH DREAMS—TO ACHIEVE YOUR GOALS!

WRITTEN UP DREAMS	*JOTTED DOWN DREAMS*

DAILY QUESTIONS TO ASK EACH OF THE DREAMS YOU HAVE:

#1.) WHAT'S MY EXPERIENCE WITH THIS DREAM FROM LAST NIGHT?

#2.) HOW DOES THIS DREAM IMPROVE THE FORCE I'M WORKING ON?

DAY THIRTY-TWO—THURSDAY—THE FEELING FORCE

I've been out of the steel business for many years; yet it still shows up in my dreams. Why do you think that is? Here is my take on it:

The purpose of dreams is to help improve the Force we are currently working on? Today I am working on the Feeling Force. So any dream I have for this day (whether about something having to do with my business of long past or something to do with my current lifestyle) is intended to help meliorate that Force.

So let's see if we can look at this first dream from last night and see how it casts some influence towards my improvement— even though the subject matter is concerned with a business I'm no longer in.

*   *   *   *

Dream #1: 'I was on the jobsite of a contractor and was given an order of steel angles for various openings in a house. I drove to our shop, got the steel angles cut to the lengths given to me and then returned to the jobsite. When the contractor started to place the angles where they went, he found he had given me the wrong lengths. I then took those angles back and brought out the correct lengths. I charged him only for the cost of the material on the first order—and then charged him for the second order—but this time including the overhead and fair profit. When I was given the lengths the second time I personally reviewed them with the contractor. I've learned if someone has made a mistake the first time he's likely to make it the second time—so that second time: he needs to be well supervised.'

What's my experience with this first dream last night?

I've always tried to be fair with builders who gave me the wrong lengths on steel angles or any wrong information that caused me an expense I could not fully bear.

I did not get upset and charge them the full price for the wrong and the right order. On the other hand I wanted them to know they had to pay a certain amount for the error they committed. But beyond that, I was glad to deal with them –as long as I made sure they got it right the second time; and to insure that, I would double check the information they gave me the second time.

But I always felt: here was a chance to build good will with such customers by treating them quite fairly and behaving without rancor.

How does this dream improve the Force I'm working on?

There may be times in the future when I'll need to recall how I acted in the steel business—with people who'd caused me an expense by giving me incorrect information. It's a chance to build up relationships while I treat folks fairly— and at the same time discipline myself in a manner, which promotes harmony in feelings that could show rancor.

Learning to coach feelings you have-- to reach free from rancor-- is a challenge folks have in every walk of life.

It's good to start early and begin to practice the drill. The trick is to train one's feelings, so there is not ever any rancor at all. It's a challenging chore, but a life of thriving should strive till the mastery's won.

This next dream is one I wanted to disregard. I may have been somewhat misled.

*   *   *   *

Dream #2: 'I took a picture of four women standing in front of Mark Twain, a local bank. I stood in front of a quite intimidating door—made fifteen feet tall by eight feet wide. As each of four succeeding doors opened, dread came over me, and I went back outside where the four women had posed. I got word that a friend had tried fishing for the first time and had gotten hurt—so he would not be coming to visit me. The women wanted to know what their assignment was, and I went off to get it.'

What's my experience with last night's second dream?

I felt in charge—photographing the four women. They were attractive; and it was easy getting the picture right.

Then I turned and tried to enter through the huge doors, but something there made me afraid. I retreated and went back to where the four stood.

Then I got word about my friend.

Really, nothing seemed to make any sense to me.

What do we do with dreams like this? It would be easy to just turn away from them.

But here's my truth: dreams mean something. But often their meaning is on a level that we are not yet able to grasp.

Have you ever thought, "How do I go from where I am (in smarts) to some place higher?"

Our brains have tremendous capacity, but if we don't stretch them, they won't expand.

The way we stretch them is to expose ourselves to situations that puzzle us. But we can't just do that for a moment or two. We have to keep on doing it.

So in this case, we have to repeat and repeat what the dream says.

What happens then? Maybe we're not ready to move up even then. But our attempts produce results.

So even if we don't come up with some way of improving our Feelings with this dream, we must always look forward to a payoff in a dream that comes along soon.

Having said all that, let's see if there is a seed for smarts that is still planted here.

Let's ask the question that we always should ask here? How does this dream improve the Force that I am working on?

Sometimes we try to do things that we are not prepared for. My trying to open those humongous portals was more than I felt safe doing.

My friend's attempt to fish-- where he had never fished—

didn't pan out safely, either.

Does this make sense to you?

Before we hurt ourselves, hopefully our Feelings will have been taught to aptly sense warnings of fearfulness. Rather than fight them, accept them.

...But here is another thought that occurs to me.

That bank is named after Mark Twain. You may know less of Twain, but I've read a fair slug of his memoirs, and they are great at showing some of the follies and lies that we smug folks inflict on each other.

But over and above much of Twain's writings, a mind strides that is full of humor-- in spite of the woes so apparent around it.

Having his name in this dream makes me think: while I regard those large doors with a fair amount of fear, I should behold them with a large amount of love

Perhaps, with love-- forces we can't lead, we'll wisely endure –as part of our challenge of being a diligent soul, striving to thrive.

...

YOUR GOALS: TO BE SMOKE-FREE AND STRIVE TO BE THRIVING

DAY#33—FRIDAY—THE THINKING FORCE

IMPROVE YOUR THINKING FORCE THROUGH DREAMS—TO ACHIEVE YOUR GOALS!

WRITTEN UP DREAMS	*JOTTED DOWN DREAMS*

DAILY QUESTIONS TO ASK EACH OF THE DREAMS YOU HAVE:

#1.) WHAT'S MY EXPERIENCE WITH THIS DREAM FROM LAST NIGHT?

#2.) HOW DOES THIS DREAM IMPROVE THE FORCE I'M WORKING ON?

DAY THIRTY-THREE—FRIDAY—THE THINKING FORCE

It's a habit of mine to use every tiny scrap of dreaming that I recall. I make it my business— although it's frustrating at times—to wring forceful values out of incomplete dreams.

You would be surprised at how something that looks like a string of worthless thoughts becomes a meaningful treasure-- after effort spent on a dream.

Here is an example of vaguely recalled thoughts— most likely—from a larger dream:

    *   *   *   *

Dream Part #1a: 'I say this: "I am out."' …
Dream Part #1b: 'Before, it seemed we went from have-nots to haves…'
Dream Part #1c: 'Later, there were witnesses of a thing being shot across the bow by some other vessel.'

My prime hunch is that the three parts I'm showing you are parts of a neglected dream.

What's my experience-- when I explore each one separately?

Let's start now, but before we do: let me briefly tell you that what I am doing here is bringing to mind any thoughts that seem to connect with the parts I'm trying to focus on.

You will be able to do the same thing with your dreams. Words in your dream will bring forth thoughts to articulate what you experience.

Let's go back to those three segments:

What's my experience with Dream Part #1a?

It looks like I have opted out. How? I've undertaken— through a stint of reading-- techniques for dream understanding. Rather than go along with them, I say: 'I'm out.' Follow me here: lots of methods exist for recording and working with one's dreams. Suppose I've spent time perusing some of them, and at last come up with my own way.

'I am out' is my reflective way of bidding 'Adieu' to how others treat dreams-- spoken not out of defiance but with humility in trying a new way.

What's my next part-experience?

I've become a "have"—with my own method—rather than a "have-not" with others' ways.

What about the third part?

Here there's a warning shot, signaling: 'Heed! Know that I'm here! I can defend myself— I mean no harm to you… as long as you're not harming me.'

How could these three segments improve the Force that I am working on? (The Thinking Force)

My sense is: these parts are fortifying my work-- opining (1) : "You're instituting a dream primer for ninth graders to learn to dream; and further(2): "In this 'new frontier' you've gone from a have-not to someone that now has." And then (3): "You are firing a shot across the bow (that is warning others to take notice of your current presence.)"

...Here's the second dream that I wrote down this past night:

   *   *   *   *

Dream #2 'Two wonderful ladies from my youngest of years appear with red hair—one's hair's more noticeable than the other's. I told one, 'Best wishes' on your son's film.'

What's my experience with last night's second dream?

Since childhood I've known these ladies. They're quite conservative-- and noticing them now with red hair seems mighty shocking.

A further surprise, too, is the success of one of the ladies' sons. Good reviews of the man's film are seen all around.

I relish seeing people or hearing of them succeeding—through their self-determination and willingness to dare to grow.

Maybe dyed red hair is a tad on the trashy side, but it is a breath of freshness.

After much acclaim, the son's film doesn't do much. But he'll be back-- trying once more.

Life's not so much about succeeding as it is about striving to thrive in life.

Having said all of that, how does this dream improve the Force that I am working on?

My thinking of others who dare to thrive in ways that may or may not succeed boostsmy determination to thrive in my own way.

And, further, my motivation in building this primer: is to show just how you can turn your dreams into guidelines that keep you smoke-free and striving to be thriving in your young lives.

But youth must try.

Don't be like those young folks who protect themselves from failure by not even trying.

The red hair and the film may not be successes, but the next thing they try just may...

Let's look at the third and final dream from last night:

    *   *   *   *

It just lasted for an instant.

Dream #3: 'I see a phone booth with a gigantic gavel propped up in it. The gavel looked big enough to be used to call for order in a large hall that's crowded with folks.'

What's my experience with this third dream last night?

I'm forced to sense that the dream is making fun of my goals. There I am with this large gavel—so big It could almost bang a large group of folks into submission, so they'd hear what I'm about to say.

How does this dream improve the Force I'm working on?

My goals for this ninth grade primer are mostly down-to-earth. I'm not seeking to fill a hall and get folks to follow all that my primer says. I am just focusing on ninth graders.

But this dream seems to be mocking that goal by showing me in a modest phone booth—yet equipped with a tool for commanding a lot of folks to hear.

I'm nowhere near that kind of goal.

I'll feel lucky if I get one soul on the phone who will listen to my message.

But perhaps--in time--my temerity blossoms, my primer gets folks' interest, and more than ninth graders soon heed what I'm saying.

It's almost too weird to repeat, but many years ago I did have a dream that came out with the following thought: "It could be that the next evolutionary step for folks is dream recording."

Regardless of whether that could ever be true, let ninth graders start keeping dreams— always on the lookout for vital messages that urge them to remain smoke-free and persuade them to start striving towards turning their lives into lives that are thriving.

YOUR GOALS: TO BE SMOKE-FREE AND STRIVE TO BE THRIVING

DAY#34—SATURDAY—THE HIGHER FEELING FORCE

IMPROVE YOUR HIGHER FEELING FORCE THROUGH DREAMS—TO ACHIEVE YOUR GOALS!

WRITTEN UP DREAMS	*JOTTED DOWN DREAMS*

DAILY QUESTIONS TO ASK EACH OF THE DREAMS YOU HAVE:

#1.) WHAT'S MY EXPERIENCE WITH THIS DREAM FROM LAST NIGHT?

#2.) HOW DOES THIS DREAM IMPROVE THE FORCE I'M WORKING ON?

DAY THIRTY-FOUR—SATURDAY—THE HIGHER FEELING FORCE

Don't be surprised if one night you have sundry dreams- while the next night, you haven't one. I have no idea why it happens that way. But having no dreams to work on allows you to catch up on the dreams you have not had time to do from dream-filled nights.

Take advantage of time you have to work on dreams You never know how a dream that you ignored at first may turn out to be a gem.

Here's one of the five dreams from last night:

* * * *

Dream #1: 'A guy tries to make me feel inferior by dismissing me from ownership in pictures of horses. He has me admit that he can better draw horses than I can. I'm a bit peeved by his showing me the necks and heads of horses that he's drawn. Their differences are just inches. The whole thing strikes me as pretty stupid.'

What's my experience with this first dream last night?

I recognized his craftsmanship, but he made me feel I was being drawn into competition I'm inept for. Maybe you've felt that way: someone challenges you to something you've not excelled in, and he declares himself the superior one.

How does this dream help to improve the Force I'm working on? (the Higher Feeling Force)

You (and I) should never let nerds drag us into contests that we aren't suited for. There are hundreds of areas of artistry; and I assure you there's at least one you'll master pretty aptly.

The point is to focus on what that just might be—rather than feel inferior—based on someone else's superiority in another field of talent. Let that guy enjoy his field—without propelling you to lament your lack therein.

Many of us spend more time getting deluged by others' gifts—than by pledging time uncovering our own.

Your dreams can serve you here. They can help you by putting you in situations and taking you to places that encourage you to see just what fields of endeavor you are talented in.

All of this comes as a bonus for your staying away from smoking and striving to live a life that is thriving.

...Here is a second dream that came to me last night: (It serves as a lesson from life.)

*   *   *   *

Dream #2: 'I walk into a small warehouse and see a guy looking at a large stack of steel cylinders. I ask him if he's interested in buying them. He tells me, "Yes." Then he asks me how much. I quote him a price that I think is fair. Then he asks me about a price for some other item. I ask my manager what I should quote. He tells me a price that I repeat to this guy. He says he'll check. All of this time— I'm feeling hesitant: I'm not sure what our costs are. So I am tentative what we should sell the stuff for. (It's such an important matter to have mastered before.)'

What's my experience with last night's second dream? (You always want to start off with that question. Asking it keeps you grounded and strong enough to keep from giving up.)

We can usually come up with some words of experience about a dream. Our Subconscious helps us when we make the effort.

The biggest fault I had when I owned a steel company was not knowing firmly what my costs were. I survived a long time in business; but not keeping costs in mind never allowed me real success. This dream helps me see that— more clearly than ever.

How does this dream improve the Force I am now working on? (the Higher Feeling Force).

This dream urges me to always comprehend what costs are. Costs do impact on all aspects of life—now and later... They can be personal...They can stalk your budgets—or any new business venture.

When a dream shows you a particular aspect of your life—now or what has passed—and it clearly makes a point you need to process—it's a way of addressing you: "You see, this is how you once were, and it's not good—so make it your job to correct it now and inculcate its correctness within: so the fault is fixed forever."

Here's the third dream I dreamed…Again, a dream that's short…and which signals a strategy.

* * * *

Dream #3: 'There was a dream where we wanted to give a guy some sauce to taste. We wanted to do him a favor as we were trying to do business with him. (It was a great sauce.)'

What's my experience with this third dream last night?

Isn't there a saying that goes: "The way to a man's heart starts off through his stomach."?

In other words, a special sauce may do wonders to get business from a prospect.

How does this dream improve the Force that I am working on?

Let's suppose I have a product (this book?), and I'm seeking pundits for approval. But they are occupied. They've not time to look at a book…But then along with the book they receive a sauce—which—perhaps—makes them more willing to take a few moments to look into the book. Would that be a cool strategy? (I could even call it Humbler Acts' Secret Sauce!)

Mind you…no sauce exists as yet. But the dream has given me a strategy for promoting this new dream primer. And it's surely given my Higher Feeling Force a shot of spunk it never had.

Here is the fourth dream that I wrote down from last night: (Again, quite a short direct one)

* * * *

Dream #4: 'I decided to get much information from an employee that I'd never gotten before—in case of an emergency. Emergencies happened before.'

What's my experience with this fourth dream last night?

How many times in business have I wanted to phone a key employee but couldn't locate his phone number? Yet, the dream might well be pointing to other times when I needed to seek out help.

How does this dream improve the Force I'm working on?

We all know that emergencies assail us all our lives. And how often are we panic-puzzled about whom we need to contract or what we ought to be doing—and we don't have any current information to help.

Doesn't this dream sort of give me a heads-up to begin thinking about people I might need to contact readily— as well as places I might well need to call?

Doesn't the dream point me towards compiling information?

Striving to thrive in life often comes down to an understanding of preparedness if something goes awry and we need to act with alacrity and confidence.

…Now here I am, retired—removed from business strife. Yet, it's still smart preparation for anything right now that I may need to know.

Do I have such information to get in touch with my family, as well as acquaintances or anyone else that I may need to get in touch with sometime?

It's something to ask myself now.

And since this dream may be useful to you, too—ask: if something were to happen now, do I have all of the information needed to deal with it? (Maybe you're not the one responsible…You will be at some point.)

It is startling how life can call upon us for something that is easy to have if only we'd prepared for it.

Here is the fifth and last dream that I dreamed last night:

(it can surely fit all of us.)

*   *   *   *

Dream #5: 'I see an old friend in the midst of doing a stand-up routine in comedy. He painted a picture of folks being reduced to buying a punk zoo to live in. As someone watching, I witness folks laughing hysterically at his humor. His timing was good, too. He also commented that when playing marbles "keep your eyes on your toes". Here was a sort of serious guy (in real life) making folks laugh.'

What's my experience with this fifth dream last night?

I was amazed: here was a guy I've literally known all of my life—as a fellow who made the most of his given abilities—now engaged in a new format—far from seriousness. And he was very good getting the crowd to laugh.

How does this dream improve the Force I am working on? (My Higher Feeling Force)

Could it be that the dream's saying: "Don't keep yourself in one tried-and-true-box. Step out. If that guy can do what he is now doing on that stage, there's no telling what you're able to do…It's important that you never shortchange yourself—just because Fate has put you in the box you're in."

Does this then mean that I ought to step on the stage—and make folks laugh? Probably not.

But it could mean that I just might be able to do something that I would never have thought that I could do—based on seeing my friend do something that I would never have thought that he could do…(Can you see yourself here?)

Most of us are not taught this way. But, in truth, the more we feed ourselves with this bold message, the more we can believe—regardless how farfetched—that we have some talents that we need to be open to.

YOUR GOALS: TO BE SMOKE-FREE AND STRIVE TO BE THRIVING

DAY#35—SUNDAY—THE HIGHER THINKING FORCE

IMPROVE YOUR HIGHER THINKING FORCE THROUGH DREAMS—TO ACHIEVE YOUR GOALS!

WRITTEN UP DREAMS	JOTTED DOWN DREAMS

DAILY QUESTIONS TO ASK EACH OF THE DREAMS YOU HAVE:

#1.) WHAT'S MY EXPERIENCE WITH THIS DREAM FROM LAST NIGHT?

#2.) HOW DOES THIS DREAM IMPROVE THE FORCE I'M WORKING ON?

DAY THIRTY-FIVE—SUNDAY—THE HIGHER THINKING FORCE

Is it too much to hope that you are still with me--as we finish with this fifth week? And is it too much to hope you're working with dreams-- according to the specific day of the week I've shown

You know, following a formal framework for fulfillment is cogent discipline for helping your life thrive.

The cultures that thrive the longest often owe their long life to the prosperity their folks get from following rules. And having you follow the format I've devised is the way to induce success for you in this primer.

Your days and Forces should follow my days and my Forces. Mondays start off the weeks, and Sundays conclude them-- just as Forces commence with the Instinctive and conclude with the Higher Thinking.

If you follow this prescribed way, you'll find that your dreams will improve each one of your Seven Forces-- according to each of the seven days of the week that you work.

Here's the first dream I dreamed last night:

*   *   *   *

Dream #1: 'I am near a golf course—when I see my son bring a couple of bags of golf clubs over to where I stand. I hadn't thought of my playing golf—since a procedure took place some months ago to repair a spinal malady. But I withdrew a number two wood and took a swing at a golf ball that was teed up. I was careful not to twist my back as I usually would—and the golf ball carried straight out and reasonably far for how I play...So I thought I could play. The credit card I used turned out to have somebody else's name on it. I went over quickly to the caddy shack and showed the guy there that I had been given someone else's credit card. He took down some information and seemed to think it would be all right.'

What's my experience with this first dream last night?

I was surprised how well I hit the golf ball, because (in real life) I'm still learning to walk again.

I was thinking I wouldn't be able to play golf much sooner than two more months, but the way I hit the ball--with little conscious effort--made me think it's fine for me to start now.

The guy's name on the card was a mentor I had not seen or heard of for ten years. He represented a street-smart philosophy that spoke of man's unawareness of his place on the earth and of man's potential for commencing to a-waken.

I felt awkward using his credit card without having gotten his approval—but maybe just having it allowed for my use.

How does this dream improve the Force that I am working on? (The Higher Thinking Force)

Golf, which I love, has now been joined to a philosophy that I greatly respect. I would never have thought the two could ever be combined.

Does this combination really improve the Force I'm on?

Like every improvement that I demonstrate in this dream primer, nothing happens instantaneously. What occurs is mostly an awareness that allows one to begin striving towards helping one's own life thrive.

When I now play golf, I'll strive to remind myself of the Earth I'm blessed to play on-- along with my obligation to become aware of what my own life might be.

One thing I would like to note here is the puzzlement that might come to some of us when we dream of people we know. People in our dreams may simply be there because they need to be part of our dream.

Just because we cannot figure out why (sometimes), doesn't mean a reason's lacking.

Here is an important attitude we need to cultivate: dreams know more than we... They are like tutors who introduce us to things that stretch our minds more than we'd like.

Our tendency in life is to avoid knowledge that we feel un-obliged to learn.

But in both cases dreams come to guide us anew.

Often we are the last on Earth to know what's good for us; then, out of the blue come dreams with stuff for guiding us forth..

Here is the second dream that I wrote down last night: (Here, too, I sensed a sort of stretch.)

   *   *   *   *

Dream #2: 'A business friend of mine mentions to me about sixteen thousand acres of land that's currently for sale. He asks me what I thought the price should be to purchase it. I tell him a price that I arrive at quickly. Later, I hear of the same land that seemed to be open for bidding from others. I struggle in my mind with how to go about bidding the right price, so we would be awarded the land ourselves.'

What's my experience with last night's second dream?

In this dream I'm ready to buy. The fact that the price for buying this acreage would amount to tens of millions doesn't seem (in the dream) to limit me too much. The deal strikes me as challenging.

How would this dream tend to improve the Force I'm on?

Like most, I think land's good to hold. But being rich enough to purchase this much land is far from my paltry bankroll.

Yet, it does no harm to have a fantastic dream.

I'm sure there are folks who once had as little as I have who one day wound up with enough cash to buy this much land.

I don't think it is a grandiose ambition that consumes me— but the point is: dreams can often project us into higher spheres of wealth, wisdom and charity that were never thought to be possible before.

There's even a thought some folks share "that all things (that man has conceived) first come through dreams". Each of us may learn that himself.

Here is the third and last dream that I dreamed last night:
*   *   *   *

Dream #3: 'A large rubber ball that I was playing with bounced over a fence—as the wind blew it into a nearby lake. By the time I got to where it had blown, it was out of my reach on dry land. I started to ask a guy if I could use his car to get to it but realized my request made no sense. With that it seemed the dream ended.'

What's my experience with this third dream last night?

Maybe some of you have had an experience like this—where the ball you're playing with blows away. A greater force takes the ball from you and leaves you hunting for it.

Like me, you try to retrieve it; and yet, like me, you find it isn't that easy...

Here-- when I ask for assistance, it makes no sense—in the circumstances involved.

How does this dream improve the Force that I'm now working on? (The Higher Thinking Force).

Even simple interruptions in our play can teach us to see: Nature's forces are events to stand in awe of.

Rather than fret about inconveniences—we might do well to recognize the dominance Nature holds. And even though we think of conquering, ultimately Nature has the last word. Life becomes more thriving when we respect Nature's power.

YOUR GOALS: TO BE SMOKE-FREE AND STRIVE TO BE THRIVING

DAY#36—MONDAY—THE INSTINCTIVE FORCE

IMPROVE YOUR INSTINCTIVE FORCE THROUGH DREAMS—TO ACHIEVE YOUR GOALS!

WRITTEN UP DREAMS	JOTTED DOWN DREAMS

DAILY QUESTIONS TO ASK EACH OF THE DREAMS YOU HAVE:

#1.) WHAT'S MY EXPERIENCE WITH THIS DREAM FROM LAST NIGHT?

#2.) HOW DOES THIS DREAM IMPROVE THE FORCE I'M WORKING ON?

DAY THIRTY-SIX—MONDAY—THE INSTINCTIVE FORCE

Come with me, now, to the first dream I dreamed last night: (You'll note I'm a bit cranky here.)

    *   *   *   *

Dream #1: 'A sales person is in my office trying to feebly sell me some frustrating information service. I ask, 'Do you send us material and then we pay for it if we want it—or do we pay for it and then you send material?' He doesn't answer me directly...I then add, 'Because I'm not paying for what I don't know I'm paying for.' (I made this kind of purchase before and wasn't pleased.)'

What's my experience with this first dream last night?

I have a bad habit of not being friendly with folks who feebly try to sell. And this dream shows me unfriendly with that brand of salesman.

I am abashed seeing the way I act. After all, the guy is trying to make a living; and he could just as well be me in years past.

Of course, I'm not off-base thoroughly questioning the product—as I always do.

My experience has been: once I buy something, it's very hard to return it. I start to feel that I just may have gotten some value from it... though in the long run, I hardly think so.

But rather than quibble with his brand of selling, why not just be polite and—at his conclusion—reject what he's selling?

There's no reason to treat him niggardly. Isn't it possible to treat salesmen like him nicely?

How does this dream improve the Force I'm working on?

I need to learn to separate salesmen from their products. Treat salesmen with respect; view products with circumspection.

I can say, 'No' to what salesmen sell, but need not treat salesmen with lack of respect. They are doing their job—there's no need to fault them. Allow them time to talk and then amicably conclude their visit once they're done.

A dream like this allows me to spot the poor self-image I show… then work with it, so my conduct becomes improved.

Always treat dreams as "friends" who want to point out to you how you can thrive much better.

Here is the second dream that I wrote down last night: (This reveals a different "me")

Please note again that my focus on myself is only so that you can begin to see how you can use your dreams—as I use mine: to improve the Force you are on.

*   *   *   *

Dream #2: 'I go up to see an old friend at his plant. We had talked of our meeting in the evening, but he was there to greet me when I arrived, which was much earlier. He introduced me to an associate, and we start talking. One thing that I recall is he wanted me to tell him what I knew of (Cuba?) Gooding and some athlete. I said that I didn't follow sports, and mentioned Gooding was an actor; and I think a stand-up comedian. Then he turned to my friend and said he liked asking people about those two to get some sense about their range of reference. Then both of these fellows sort of disappeared, as I was worrying about picking back up something I'd set on a ledge at the end of the plant. But after a spell of hesitation, I tried to follow where they had gone. As I tried opening a door leading outside, I was appalled at the sight of flaked-off paint on the door.'

What's my experience with last night's second dream?

I get upset with my habit of scarcely focusing on people's names when they are introduced to me quickly.

I think recalling names is a skill that most of us fail to groom, miserably.

The only cue that helps me-- when I observe it— is to connect the person's first name to the same name of someone I'm already familiar with. But in this case, I never bothered to do that-- with the name of my friend's partner or the name of the athlete he mentioned.

How I'd love to program myself to make introduced folks a "memorable event"—each and every time.

I have mentioned remembering names before, and I urge you to master this task-- if you really do little else. It will tend to make your smoke-free life quite thriving.

How does this dream help to improve the Force I'm working on?

I need to make this Force (The Instinctive) into a Force to remember folks' names whatever the instance.

It may be that Cuba Gooding's name could be turned into "Cue be good thing"-- that is: when I hear the name of someone, make that name "cue" into something that recalls it—a skill that would be a "good thing".

Here is the last dream that I wrote down from last night: (Right now I am puzzled with it.)

*   *   *   *

Dream #3: 'I'm talking to the head of a small private school. I've just reviewed all the steel that will be needed—as far as I can see on the structural plans he has shown me. But he quickly points out two places that also need to get steel. I was a bit embarrassed, but when I searched I could not find an indication that steel went there. I may not have made a deft effort to find it. I did make a remark that the school did not care enough about math to include it now in its curriculum.'

What's my experience with this third dream last night?

It doesn't show me in a light I can proudly bask in. I came off as a poor estimator of quantities of steel-- needed on plans.

[135]

And then I put my two cents worth in what's not my business.

Do I tend to do that? Frankly, I'm not aware, but often dreams point out matters that we're oblivious to recognize, ourselves.

How does this dream help me improve the Force I'm working on? (still: the Instinctive Force)

It reveals an unconscious ploy in getting around an inadequacy by criticizing someone else's.

…Not a good thing if one wants a life that's thriving.

Whether you see it or you don't, everything that you are doing here points to the importance of using dreams to improve your Forces: so "all of you" will be fit to circumvent starting smoking.

YOUR GOALS: TO BE SMOKE-FREE AND STRIVE TO BE THRIVING

DAY#37—TUESDAY—THE SEXUAL FORCE

IMPROVE YOUR SEXUAL FORCE THROUGH DREAMS—TO ACHIEVE YOUR GOALS!

WRITTEN UP DREAMS	*JOTTED DOWN DREAMS*

DAILY QUESTIONS TO ASK EACH OF THE DREAMS YOU HAVE:

#1.) WHAT'S MY EXPERIENCE WITH THIS DREAM FROM LAST NIGHT?

#2.) HOW DOES THIS DREAM IMPROVE THE FORCE I'M WORKING ON?

DAY THIRTY-SEVEN—TUESDAY—THE SEXUAL FORCE

Here's the only dream (last night) I recalled to write: (Often a dream disappoints us.)

*   *   *   *

Dream #1: 'There's a dream where I am trying to firm up a date to go to a movie with someone in my family…Whoever that is, I'm promised that we'll go tomorrow night. Tomorrow comes, and other plans have been made. Also, there are two restaurants next door to each other—but only one has a person to wait on customers. I happen to have a vanilla cone from one place and want to get something else at the other place, but cannot. I try to serve myself going around the back.'

What's my experience with this one dream last night?

There's a sense of disappointment.

I love going to a movie…I'm almost like a kid—as I look forward with keen anticipation— Perhaps, more with that than the actual movie, itself.

So when the date ends up cancelled, I feel a bit let down—but then, it's no big deal. Something else fills the gap; and the disappointment is forgotten.

Experiencing the fiasco with the two restaurants almost seemed ludicrous. Having been in business myself—and having witnessed screw-ups that every business makes—I simply note that the parties running these two restaurants dropped the ball somewhere.

Again, it's no big deal—yet, it simply detracts from the pleasant experience I would have-- if things had been better organized.

In dealing with the way I felt: this weak dream reminded me of a stronger dream— one that advised me to react to life's disappointments with a simple saying-- a saying that I've found helpful. Just repeating it does seem to turn a moment of frustration into something that's scarcely bothersome.

…Perhaps you will have a stronger dream, too…or you're

welcome to use the one that's here: (It may strike you as weird— but words like these ease displeasure:)

'Learn: SO BE IT...ENDURE'

Maybe you can use it— when little things go wrong for you.

How does this dream improve the Force I'm working on?

Often our plans emerge awry-- with the Sexual Force. Things get planned—like going to a "movie", and then one of our twosome has to put the kibosh on the plan. It is normal to get upset.. Similarly, we may be disgruntled with a "cone" and nothing to go with it.

Whether truth's in this thought-- or simply randomness—I do try to trust that in life: there's integral design in all that impedes us. And if others cannot serve us, then we have to learn how to best serve our own needs. It really does not matter what we decide we will do— as long as we do not injure ourselves or hurt others.

Such a dream--as this one--confirms what some have sensed: (especially when there is no one around to really give the correct guidance): dreams mature us, sexually. And with that may well come a newfound self-esteem.

A number of folks, I suspect, sorely feel lost with the prospect of thriving with the Sexual Force as shown here.

How can ninth graders thrive when adult mentors may themselves lust in total darkness—never quite knowing what or how to deal with sex?

Dreams may help most folks start to see just what their roles should be with their Sexual Force.

If dreams present themes that may be uncomfortable to grasp, it may be the dream's way of getting us awakened and forcing us to learn much more about this Force.

One aspect of new knowledge might be learning that early smoking persists, because young folks fondle their cigarettes and embrace addiction as an escape from a wholesome thriving with the Sex Force.

Kids start smoking at an age when their bodies push undue thoughts towards sex energy. Putting that energy into smoking crudely appears to curb much discomfort.

But there's nothing like a fresh appreciation of what this Force is all about. Even if we never know exactly what dreams tell us about our own Sex Force, we may still get a glimpse of truth— once we've practiced asking what our experience with our dream is and then asking how the dream does improve the Force we're working on.

…Let me once again raise a question that may still trouble you: "How do we know that sleep-dreams we have for that day will have a thing to do with our own Sexual Force?"

My experience is: a "connection's" been set up—based on trust that may exist between our Sexual Force and our newly found dream life—just as this trust exists between other Forces and the self-same dream life.

I affirm that trust may exist-- whether it's something that you can affirm, as well— through your own dream observations — or whether you will think it's totally absurd—depends on your experience.

I hope your efforts do or will affirm that trust.

YOUR GOALS: TO BE SMOKE-FREE AND STRIVE TO BE THRIVING

DAY#38—WEDNESDAY—THE MOVING FORCE

IMPROVE YOUR MOVING FORCE THROUGH DREAMS—TO ACHIEVE YOUR GOALS!

WRITTEN UP DREAMS	*JOTTED DOWN DREAMS*

DAILY QUESTIONS TO ASK EACH OF THE DREAMS YOU HAVE:

#1.) WHAT'S MY EXPERIENCE WITH THIS DREAM FROM LAST NIGHT?

#2.) HOW DOES THIS DREAM IMPROVE THE FORCE I'M WORKING ON?

DAY THIRTY-EIGHT—WEDNESDAY—THE MOVING FORCE

Have you ever dreamed a dream followed by one more—on and on—yet never thought of writing down one of them? That happened to me last night; and I can't explain how it came about. It is as if laziness conquered any wish to remember dreams.

It was only towards the time when I woke up that I had this dream that I wrote down:

    *   *   *   *

Dream #1: 'I got involved in a tremendous prize award that made me feel quite uneasy. Two friends of mine entered a contest and won it rightfully. But another two friends somehow entered past the expiration date for entering –yet somehow they wound up being declared winner. However, it had never been officially announced that the second couple was the winner. I happened to know about it and felt almost guilty and uncomfortable. But my two friends were not. I took them aside and warned them that the other couple was going to raise all kinds of hell when they learned that their great prize had been stolen. But these winners were not concerned. I couldn't quite get that. A lot of money was attached to the prize.

…Later, a group of us were going to sit at a picnic-like table; and I just seemed to wait for other folks to arrive there before I decided where I'd like to sit.'

What's my experience with this one dream last night?

When I reflect on how I looked in this dream—reluctant to desert scofflaw friends— and timid with choosing a seat at a picnic table— I have to admit that I seemed to be hiding myself behind the behavior that I manifested. Is this the way I want to act?

How does this dream improve the Force I'm working on? (The Moving Force is where we are.)

One of the goals that dreams invite us to work on is genuine right behavior that we should undertake.

Is "timid" how I act in my dealings with other folks?

Do I want to remain the sort of person that never takes a stand that might risk his comfort or others' displeasure or rebuke?

Some might call that a "gentleman"— and in my own mind I think of myself as that. But is that the way I should act? Certainly, one doesn't risk too much being that.

But what about one's inner self? Is it developing a way that forges the Force, here, into harmony with the other Six Forces?

If I stay as I am in the above mentioned dream scene— recognizing that here's a chance for me to change-- is it the right behavior for the rest of my Forces— or could there be a kind of imbalance or frustration that this behavior casts on the other Forces?

Certainly, I don't want to act out in a way that harms the life I want to live...

So I review this dream and try to see how it improves the Force I'm working on, asking myself those questions— while again recognizing an opportunity…

Here are the turns I wish to take: (Mind you: such changes don't happen in an instant.).

I need to stand for something. That may not be what will get me all the friends I'd like— and it may force me to tarnish the quiet harmony that I am striving for— but in the end it should create the kind of consummate thriving life that I wish.

Such thoughts may be rare innermost ones that dreams urge us to exercise—a process that we might not ever think of engaging in—had a dream not set us thinking.

Taking the time to reflect on your dreams—by writing down your thoughts as I have done with mine—will set you on a path that's quite fulfilling and reaches higher paths than most others you may have followed.

Here's the really crucial part of this whole process: you're obliged to be honest with yourself... How often are you encouraged that way?

Life may train us dishonestly: Mentors might have taught us to act dissembling ways—to even think dissembling thoughts. Yet, it's practical for us to heed what they say. We can't grow like wild animals— misacting early on without any training.

But once we are in the ninth grade—it may be time to spend moments each day searching through our dreams with each new day's Force-- becoming passionate for the grand goals we seek

...Now ask yourself these three questions:

How many kids your age take up smoking without the faintest thought of what they do?

How many just pick up a cigarette and light it—expecting each flawed puff to immediately transform them into a cool, well-endowed adventurer?

Does any kid ever examine all the "cons", publicizing why not to smoke? You don't have to weigh the cons—using this program.

You just let your dreams start to show you what your life is now— and guide you to learn how you ought to thrive in wiser ways..

YOUR GOALS: TO BE SMOKE-FREE AND STRIVE TO BE THRIVING

DAY#39—THURSDAY—THE FEELING FORCE

IMPROVE YOUR FEELING FORCE THROUGH DREAMS—TO ACHIEVE YOUR GOALS!

WRITTEN UP DREAMS	*JOTTED DOWN DREAMS*

DAILY QUESTIONS TO ASK EACH OF THE DREAMS YOU HAVE:

#1.) WHAT'S MY EXPERIENCE WITH THIS DREAM FROM LAST NIGHT?

#2.) HOW DOES THIS DREAM IMPROVE THE FORCE I'M WORKING ON?

DAY THIRTY-NINE—THURSDAY—THE FEELING FORCE

This night I awakened with a stretch of dread that something was just not going right--as far as how I was disclosing dreams to you.

Weren't the dreams I was now having replete with grave warnings that I ought to divulge? I couldn't tell, but without one dream spelling out its theme -- I felt driven to write a long comment from my bedside:

'I've begun to feel uneasy in my preaching ways of behaving. These things I dream are for me alone. I'm only giving them as examples. Your mode of conduct and your path may be different. One of the things that has caused our world to be dangerous is that men come up with strong rituals that they then push upon others. Often what they have been led to believe may be only for them --not for everyone else. I believe dreams are meant for the dreamer alone. I would not want others to take my dreams and apply them— without seeing what their dreams are. Yes—perhaps mine are fair as models—but let each dreamer come up with his own dreams.'

My hope is that you will learn two things from your dreams:

1.) How to live a life that's thriving.

2.) How to be strong enough to refrain from smoking.

How will you know how to succeed?

A lot of your success may come in ways that you cannot explain. When dreams help you lift your overall self to a lofty platform where talent you have is revealed-- and you begin having true recognition of yourself and the balance of life--it will be then that there will be no way on earth that you will seek after smoking.

…Here is the lone dream that I recalled from last night: (It's a new kind of dream for me.)

*   *   *

Dream #1:'There's a large patch of soil with a few blades of grass poking up. I think that when I look at a lawn full of grass, I am looking at thousands of such blades all growing—so thick together it looks more like a carpet than those thousands of blades of grass.'

What's my experience with this one dream last night?

It struck me: I'm comprehending a brand new awareness of Nature's genius. (How strange that thought appears unique!)

How does this dream improve the Force I'm working on?

We're progenies of Nature; and realizing the grand phenomena that are all around us should encourage our minds and hearts to strive as nobly as they can.

So often we become absorbed with trivial short takes that cannot nourish us. So in this dream I'm reminded of one thing around me (the miracle of grass) that, hopefully, lifts my spirits a little higher than they might normally rise.

When you have a dream such as this, it can often happen you'll see more in a few blades of grass than ever before.

Don't be opposed to pass a few moments building a narrative from such a dream. For instance, we are all like a few blades of grass-- poking up in a field of soil that needs thousands of blades of grass to be verdant.

Each move that we make to improve is like bringing forth a single new blade of grass. If we keep on-- never flagging--and finding enough rest to continue onwards-- at some point we'll consecrate the ground that no longer shows soil but is filled with grass.

You may scoff at such sentiment, but as you fill your mind and heart—as I'm filling mine—with such thoughts— of hallowed field-- you'll find yourself able to steer clear of any smoking habits.

I think some folks react restlessly when they wake up from

a dream-- probably a carryover from when they were youngsters and reported a dream— only to hear somebody else pooh-pooh that dream and tell them never to give thought to it again. ("Dreams are rubbish."?)

Yet, a few lucky folks have grown up—believing it is a huge disservice when children have been taught that their dreams have no value…Their dreams are mere mental garbage.(?)

It's such an injustice to the genius of dreams to banish them in such a way.

Hopefully, at some point, a recognition of dreams will become prominent in the minds of parents and of all adult mentors; and tots' psychic health will improve..

In the meantime, now's the perfect time for youngsters in the ninth grade to start the ball rolling by beginning to appreciate the value of dreams and their insights-- to reach goals that are now being prescribed for them.

Perhaps they will be the future parents who have the sense to encourage their kids to share their dreams during childhood.

YOUR GOALS: TO BE SMOKE-FREE AND STRIVE TO BE THRIVING

DAY#40—FRIDAY—THE THINKING FORCE

IMPROVE YOUR THINKING FORCE THROUGH DREAMS—TO ACHIEVE YOUR GOALS!

WRITTEN UP DREAMS	*JOTTED DOWN DREAMS*

DAILY QUESTIONS TO ASK EACH OF THE DREAMS YOU HAVE:

#1.) WHAT'S MY EXPERIENCE WITH THIS DREAM FROM LAST NIGHT?

#2.) HOW DOES THIS DREAM IMPROVE THE FORCE I'M WORKING ON?

DAY FORTY—FRIDAY—THE THINKING FORCE

Forty days together! Are you having fun yet?

For those of you who have tried hard to follow what I've shown, I am cheering for you!

Some of you may have quickly glanced over this dream primer before trying it out— and then maybe, "It's not for me."

…Life is filled with all sorts of ninth grader pathways; and this primer's surely not for all ninth graders out there. But for those of you who are attracted to what is here, let me go over a method of approach I strongly suggest that you support.

First: strive to inculcate the idea that you are made up of Seven Forces. Strive to commit them to memory and welcome them as part of your own being.

Next: associate all dreams that you have to the particular Force of the week.

By now you've read many dreams and have been shown how I believe they can help improve the Force you're working on.

Have you been able to try my method with your own dreams? Even if you have not been able to find in your dreams worthy connections with the Force you're working on and improveing, take faith in knowing that it may take time-- just like any other new activity—to get the hang of how to do it.

The method that I have developed comes from my admiration for two men who published valuable insights regarding the conditions they found in human beings. One man, Sigmund Freud, discovered that the dreams his patients were having showed a distinct connection between the illnesses they suffered from and the treatment that might help them improve. Freud was the founder of Psychiatry.

I have taken Freud's general findings and tried to apply them to how dreams might help young people to simply get a grip on dealing with their lives.

But dreams on their own can only be of limited worth-- unless they are moored to some aspect of being human.

That special need was filled by taking note of what another man, G.I. Gurdjieff, discovered in his work with all types of people. He found that they are all governed by the Seven Forces, which he named as follows: The Instinctive, The Sexual, The Moving, The Feeling, The Thinking, The Higher Feeling and the Higher Thinking.

Each one of these Forces, he found, has a direct bearing on how human beings conduct their lives. He learned-- through the experience of others as well as himself—that a person cannot really be a full-fledged person until he or she has been able to bring each one of these Forces up to a level that makes them whole.

By combining both Freud's and Gurdjieff's grand insights, a modest thought was brought to mind for helping ninth graders begin to deal with their lives as they face the challenges that test them as they grow from youth towards adulthood.

In my mind, their main challenges are: to avoid smoking and to undertake to live lives that are fully thriving.

But it is crucial not to underestimate the importance of the Seven Forces, and how any one of them can do great damage to our overall lives.

We see all around us examples of young folks letting one Force take over and totally destroy the other Forces fiercely.

Drug addiction is an exact example of how the Instinctive Force becomes prey to power of drugs and takes the rest of the Forces often to their demise.

The Sexual Force, unleashed, can drive youth into crises that cause its raw downfall and undo the other Forces.

Learning to educate these Forces through our dreams

seems a prudent way to avoid many of fate's pitfalls as well as to build a life that's thriving for each of us.

About the only thing that I have done is to put dreams and the Forces into the seven days of the week, so as to construct a sequential method for growth.

My hope is that my small contribution will give ninth graders a way of delving into their own Forces in a positive way and coming out with new insights into how they can find the best roads to travel and the byways they should avoid.

By all means, those of you who have questions can reach me by e-mail, phone or snail mail:

Humbler Acts @ aol.com
Humbler Acts—314-574-7681
Humbler Acts
900 South Hanley Road
Unit 1-E
Clayton, MO 63105
USA

I had the following dream last night, which I now would like to show and comment on:

   *   *   *   *

Dream #1:'Some lady's accepted my book (or manuscript) and told me she had put a long line above it. When I mentioned her words to my sister, she showed a sweet greeting of enthusiasm. I ask her, 'Is that good?' "Oh, yes!" she said. (I wasn't sure-- let alone familiar-- with what such a mark meant. It seemed to spark a beginning.'

What's my experience with this one dream last night?

Naturally, everyone likes to get feedbacks that ring positive for one's work.

That a dream is the source of such feedback is, hopefully, a harbinger for what positive words others may say—once this dream primer is released out in the world.

How does this dream improve the Force I am now working

on?

My Thinking Force always bows to words and acts of people who approve what I've done. Like food to the stomach are words and acts to the Thinking.

Whenever you find your dreams supporting your work, you can be sure you'll grow stronger.

Of course, there's no success that doesn't come without challenges that echo folks' "No's". That is part of the world and will always be there.

As long as you work from within and remain strong without, rest assured you'll succeed.

Regardless how big or how small— what tales of success from dreams have you to report? I'd be thrilled to hear what they are.

YOUR GOALS: TO BE SMOKE-FREE AND STRIVE TO BE THRIVING

DAY#41—SATURDAY—THE HIGHER FEELING FORCE

IMPROVE YOUR HIGHER FEELING FORCE THROUGH DREAMS—TO ACHIEVE YOUR GOALS!

WRITTEN UP DREAMS	*JOTTED DOWN DREAMS*

DAILY QUESTIONS TO ASK EACH OF THE DREAMS YOU HAVE:

#1.) WHAT'S MY EXPERIENCE WITH THIS DREAM FROM LAST NIGHT?

#2.) HOW DOES THIS DREAM IMPROVE THE FORCE I'M WORKING ON?

DAY FORTY-ONE—SATURDAY—THE HIGHER FEELING FORCE

Here's the first dream I had and worked on from last night: (Here you'll see how a dream sometimes stakes us to a new role that elicits response from us to help improve our Force.)

*   *

Dream #1: 'Here I am trying to sell a house to a guy. I have numbers that a while back I assembled on the house, and I'm trying to work on the sale again. I'm in a hurry to bring in two real estate salesmen. I go over the price and a little bit on the house features. The prospective buyer has a number that is much lower than mine. What am I to do? Try to see if we can negotiate?

What's my experience with this first dream last night?

It's surprising how dreams stake us to roles we've never played. It's as if the dream source designated: "You're the actor…Now see how you behave; now see about other actors you've got to contend with…Now see if you've learned from this what you should not do."

Before I learn, though, let me dwell on the experience that I had with this dream:

I didn't feel smartly prepared. I did have figures for what I wanted to sell the house for-- as well as features that I could boast about. But my notes were marked on brown paper with a plain pencil. The look was far from a professional sales page. And I behaved pretty slipshod.

Doesn't a good salesman take his time, get the pulse of the buyer and most likely emphasize all of the great values in the house before talking about the price?

… And surely confusion reigns when two real estate fellows arrive. Wasn't I one? Or maybe it's my house?

Weren't the figures old ones? In the dream I thought I had put down all the facts from a couple of years ago. But facts about a house can change. Maybe a new roof is needed as well as paint?

On a scale of one to ten, I would rate myself a three in terms of sales prowess.

If I had to "dream" this again, shouldn't I check recent sales figures and price and have on hand first-rate brochures... as well as query the buyer on what he wants?.

How does this dream help me improve the Force I'm working on?

The most important thing in selling—or so I should think—is ascertaining what the buyer is thinking. The next is to relax and let a relationship start. Third: convince the buyer subtly that I'm successful in the role I'm now playing.

He may differ from me…He may have on worn-out clothing and behave stupidly. Yet, that might be his choice.

Mine is to be professional. So I've got to be set to succeed in that role.

The "best-in-show" folks in this world all appear to be well prepared in their careers. They spend hours getting ready. That's what I need to do .

Perhaps the dream is meant for you as well in that all of us are obliged to play the role of salesperson--as we try to convince others to "buy" what we're selling-- even if it's ourselves.

*   *   *   *   *

The next dream states what I should do:

Dream #2: 'I recall a dream where I'm saying that as a person ages he has a much harder time expressing his feelings. The reason (I mention this) is that he no longer possesses the vocabulary to express feelings. Also feelings have gotten weaker with age. I must have been in front of others as I said this.'

What's my experience with last night's second dream?

Some years ago I had this short dream: "Learn twelve words a day." I've tried to follow that, but I can't say I always did.

Why would anyone try to learn twelve words a day?

Whether or not you've thought about it before, the best way we can express ourselves to others or even think thoughts is by having in our minds enough words to state properly how we feel or think.

If we only rely on four letter words or cast-off clichés, which have lost their meanings from senseless use, we'll never convince folks that we're people to listen to.

The more words we can learn to be able to think and express, the better chance we have to communicate and be counted in life.

Of course, I doubt that most of us will remember all the words that we strive to learn. Yet our minds are quite receptive in implementing our wish to improve word-use by helping us communicate much better to others.

How does this dream improve the Higher Force I'm working on?

I think it's warning me to make sure I don't let age rob me of the will to keep learning twelve words a day— lest I be unable to express my feelings (and thoughts).

As a notice to ninth graders: I am convinced that words are one area that everybody needs to take an interest in. Next to making an effort in remembering people's names, comes being able to express one's thoughts and feelings.

*   *   *   *   *

Here is the next dream that appeared to me last night: (It's repugnant yet eloquent.)

Dream #3: 'I witness a scene where a rat is overhead— walking on a large steel framework. Then as I get out of its way—it drops onto the concrete floor. At that moment a grisly looking bear appears. The bear spots the rat and in an instant seizes it in his mouth. I watch- slightly horrified- as the bear trembles mightily with his jaws as he grips the rat and slowly drags it into his throat. It's a bloody scene—yet I don't stand that far away as it dies. The rat's tail was the last to go.'

What's my experience with this third dream last night?

This looked as real as real can get. As a matter of fact, when I recollect that I have never ever witnessed anything like this scene, I have to wonder how does a dream "dream up" such a dream? Where does the source of dreams beget such gruesome stuff?

You might say, "Well, you imagined the whole thing by yourself!" But that's hard to conceive. How would I know to come up with a bear trembling as it firmly grips on a rat? And the scene with the blood is not something I could concoct..

This is something that must give us pause, if we deride dreams as something meaningless. My sense is that dreams come from a Divine Reality that exists around us--- and depending on what dreams need to say, they draw from that Divine Reality.

I suspect that there are inventions out there waiting for the right time and the right person or persons to bring them to light. You might be one of those persons, yourself.

How did this dreadful dream help me improve the Force I'm on? (The Higher Feeling Force)

If nothing else, it helps me realize the power that dreams wield for all of us. While dreams show killing, they may greet us with grander things, too.

For me personally, I soon saw quite clearly that the rat was "overhead" and a threatening presence that slowly ground me down— forcing me to close my business.

When I got out of the rat's way-- before it fell--the bear was there to consume it.

…In life I've learned: owners should manage a business with the 'barest' of expenses.

You may laugh or smirk at my interpretation of this dream,

but If I could draw or paint, I would show the moment when the bear caught the rat, frame the scene and hang it--as a reminder for controlling overhead.

*   *   *   *   *

Here's the fourth dream I dreamed last night:

Dream #4: 'I find myself with a group of young women. There must have been some sort of dancing that was going on. One lady tapped me on the back of my neck as if cutting in on me. Next, I was about to tap the neck of a lady who had freckles.'

What's my experience with this fourth dream last night?

I am starting out totally stumped by this dream-- as to what my experience really is. For sure I am not confronted by a foe who is life threatening --and perhaps there is playfulness in my tapping someone after I have been tapped.

Certainly, I have to ask, 'What am I doing in there? Is there anything there that makes meaning or sense to me?'

Asking myself over and over those questions, I would have to say, 'I don't know.' Wouldn't it be better if I could say, 'I'm there in order to "blah, blah" something.'?

How does this dream improve the Force I'm working on?

So often in life we're engrossed and doing something; and we never stop to think 'Why am I here—What is my goal?'

We simply are someplace, because we find ourselves there—and we don't ever dare ask ourselves anything more.

Perhaps this dream intends to point out to me that often-- or maybe most often-- in my life I am with others, doing things and never quite consciously asking myself what or why I'm experiencing what's going on.

That may sound silly, but shouldn't we be able to verbally explain ourselves as we live out our lives?. How many of us have been in places or with others and been real lucky to get out of there alive or at least with little harm—

and all because we never asked ourselves, 'Why am I doing this thing or being with this particular group?'

Perhaps, "asking" is what I (maybe you) should start doing in real life; and then it might follow that we will ask the question, similarly, when we have a dream where we find ourselves in strange surroundings with folks we don't know.

*   *   *   *   *

Here is the fifth and last dream that I had last night: (Let's see where growth may come from here)

Dream #5: 'I happen to notice a man and a woman embracing and could somehow see that a saliva drop fell from his throat onto her tongue and how she then drew her tongue in to absorb it. I watched the same thing happen three times just like the first.'

What's my experience with this last dream last night?

It looked to me just like nectar dropping from one to the other. Was it sacred--.a ritual, they're performing?. Being privy to the scene fascinated me.

So how does this dream improve the Force I'm working on?

When two people can share something that's so intimate and—except for me-- unseen by leering spectators, could that make them soulfully one? Could it really happen that two could become one?

I've never quite believed they could—but seeing this dream and seeing how two relate, I'm beginning to think they could.

Perhaps lovers are like bees pollinating—but unlike those bees pollinating flowers, these "human bees" strive to pollinate each other... and that substance flows on to each one of their souls—breeding benign bondage.

A whole new realm of thriving grows within me. A beauty that has been foreign to me emerges and brings a new enlightenment for how two people can exist in a world meant to share love in.

Here is an insight which is so pure one's smoking in any form would erase it.

YOUR GOALS: TO BE SMOKE-FREE AND STRIVE TO BE THRIVING

DAY#42—SUNDAY—THE HIGHER THINKING FORCE

IMPROVE YOUR HIGHER THINKING FORCE THROUGH DREAMS—TO ACHIEVE YOUR GOALS!

WRITTEN UP DREAMS	*JOTTED DOWN DREAMS*

DAILY QUESTIONS TO ASK EACH OF THE DREAMS YOU HAVE:

#1.) WHAT'S MY EXPERIENCE WITH THIS DREAM FROM LAST NIGHT?

#2.) HOW DOES THIS DREAM IMPROVE THE FORCE I'M WORKING ON?

DAY FORTY-TWO—SUNDAY—THE HIGHER THINKING FORCE

Here is the first dream that I dreamed from this past night. It's a teaching dream that touched me.

* * * *

Dream #1: 'I'm talking with someone who is in a study work program that will allow him to serve veterans who have become handicapped due to their stay in combat zones where terrible events unfolded before them. I began to learn how these folks were being taught how to revise their attitudes about how they need to live now. It's hard to imagine what it would be like to find yourself with no arms or legs after a short lifetime of having them intact . What a challenge they all must have not only to face their new lives with the anguish of sacrifice but with the thought that maybe the war they fought was never needed. That must be a war of its own.'

What's my experience with this first dream last night?

Through dreams, we are often able to express thoughts and strong feelings that in real life we have managed to long postpone.

Certainly, I've mourned in silence for brave warriors; and my sense of how wars are waged is one of grim despair, but what I've dreamed above aroused feelings of grave sadness.

How does this dream improve the Force I'm working on?

I think it is crucial for me to see reality in the most honest way. If I just go along and have no affiliation with war's harsh sufferings, am I not then denying truth?

I should be able to behold the nightmare of wars that persist throughout the world.

Dreams bestow naivete to speak truth about war. Do those of us who sense this truth need to start working the front lines to help soldiers who have suffered from savage wars?

My consciousness adds to the awareness of the earth: that wars should never be waged.

If ninth graders could think in this forthright manner, perhaps, there would be a groundswell of sentiment that would deflect the course of wars and promote some war-substitutes.

No one's yet proposed what substitutes can be found— or that some might be imagined, but that substitutes may be the answer none should ever deny or dare dispute.

At least for me my dream summons the heartfelt wish that others might dream on further..

*   *   *   *

Here's another dream that teaches emboldenly. Is this something you can learn from?

Dream #2: 'I'm away at Oxford where we're required to wear loose fitting black vests during all forms of classes that occur during the day. There seems to be a shortage of vests and for some reason at the end of the day students hand them in at stations. Because of the shortage, the problem is finding one each day. A fellow student is very helpful in trying to locate one for me. Having found one he can wear, he is spending his time searching for one for me. His is the act of a friend.'

What's my experience with last night's second dream?

The shortage of vests at Oxford isn't quite accurate, but in the dream it is represented as a problem.

I was gratefully moved by this fellow student's act of friendship in helping me. I recognized him but couldn't recall his name.

I did recall a wide table that had some bearing on whether a vest lay there.

How does this dream improve the Force that I am working on?

I gathered from the word 'vest': that each day folks needed to latch on to a new vest i.e. "become vested" in some sort of act of friendship.

"Hold on!" you might exclaim. "That is pretty far-fetched!" (Even if it's far-fetched, it fits!)

The fact that the guy is helping me find a vest is like someone telling me, "You, too, need to be vested in some act of friendship."

Since by nature I am not one who does daily acts of friendship (My wife seems to be the one who represents us in that category) the purpose of this dream is to improve that deficit by helping me become vested every day in doing some act of friendship.

Is not this a daunting dream for me to deal with? Yet isn't life thriving with it?

As I asked at the start, can you learn from this, too?

What do you say if we both try?

*   *   *   *

The next dream also has me involved with Oxford. Let's try to search for its purpose.

Dream #3: 'Some guy asks me where I went to college; and I tell him it was The Queen's College, Oxford. He asks if I went to see it before I enrolled. I tell him that was sixty years ago, and it was a big deal to go over to England from the U.S. for a visit—five days aboard a ship. It wasn't like the visits made to U.S. colleges by plane by folks today.(It probably wouldn't have hurt.)'

What's my experience with this third dream last night?

I objected to what he asked. I responded as if such a visit would not have made much sense. I excused my lack of a visit on the great distance involved. Belatedly, I saw his point.

How does this dream improve the Force I'm working on?

I wouldn't trade my Oxford life for anything, but the truth was I wasted a lot of time there that I might have more wisely spent elsewhere.

I had a tendency to rush to get into Oxford; and no one dared challenge me as to how Oxford would play out in my future life.

I think the dream is right in its evoking: that surely-- if I had visited Oxford before being a student there-- I might have assessed it with more foresight.

But history is what's past; and I believe what's past always boosts one's present value.

And today's value in this dream: is proposing I spend much more time reflecting before undertaking far afield adventures.

Again, a dream has brought to mind what I've not admitted yet needed to be told-- in order to improve this Force.

 *   *   *   *

Here is the fourth dream that I encountered last night.
Every dream helps us in some way.

Dream #4: ' A recently deceased friend comes into a space where I'm watching a sports event on TV. There are folks all around— most of them not paying much attention to the telecast. My friend takes a chair and tries his best to make sure he does not block my vision—as he sits slightly in front of me and to the left of where I am.'

What's my experience with this fourth dream last night?

When he entered the room, I'm not sure I thought he was dead. It's possible I did, but in dreams it's unlikely one cries: 'Holy cow! He's dead! This is really eerie!' No such thought seems to come to mind.

Dreams scarcely show concern with a dead friend's visit. As far as I could tell, he came in and wanted to watch the sports event with me.

He showed he is considerate by making sure-- when he sat down-- he wouldn't block my vision from what I'm watching.

How does this dream improve the Force I'm working on?
(It's the Higher Thinking Force.)

I speculate that this dream is using my dead friend's visit simply to inform me that the dead don't visit to block our vision of how the real world's competitive-- but they visit just to help share what we're seeing.

Their spirits live on after death, but they live on in us and not out there in space.

We should welcome them in our dreams as companions that our unconscious mind wants us to benefit from in some way. In this case my friend just wanted to tell me that he's not there to block my vision--but only to serve as a friendly companion.

Our lives become more thriving when we cognize that visits such as this are sources for improving the Force we're on.

YOUR GOALS: TO BE SMOKE-FREE AND STRIVE TO BE THRIVING

DAY#43—MONDAY—THE INSTINCTIVE FORCE

IMPROVE YOUR INSTINCTIVE FORCE THROUGH DREAMS—TO ACHIEVE YOUR GOALS!

WRITTEN UP DREAMS	JOTTED DOWN DREAMS

DAILY QUESTIONS TO ASK EACH OF THE DREAMS YOU HAVE:

#1.) WHAT'S MY EXPERIENCE WITH THIS DREAM FROM LAST NIGHT?

#2.) HOW DOES THIS DREAM IMPROVE THE FORCE I'M WORKING ON?

DAY FORTY-THREE—MONDAY—THE INSTINCTIVE FORCE

Here are two golf dreams that I wrote down from last night. Certainly, they're a change of pace.

    *   *   *   *

Dream #1: 'There was a ten foot wide by ten foot long carpet (on the driveway where my steel firm once existed). It was black and white and had folds in it. A friend of mine (a first-rate golfer) said something about the golf pro's pledge that he'd give a lesson on this carpet rain or shine. I asked when his lesson was. He said at twelve thirty. I was to have mine at twelve noon. (There was something about this whole thing that didn't make sense.)'

What's my experience with this first dream last night?

I had to muse during this dream:

'What a strange place to take a golf lesson, and what a peculiar kind of surface to take the lesson on. And for a pro to pledge to give lessons-- regardless of whether it rains or shines...talk about frivolous!'

How could this dream improve the Force I am now working on? (It's the Instinctive Force.)

As you may not have known yet, I'm recovering from a spinal operation. Everything's getting better, but it takes time to get back to activities that I once could do normally.

I've been thinking about starting to play some golf, which I haven't played for some time.

This dream brings up the thought of my taking lessons; which is a smart way to start back. But why all the wacky aspects mixed in with it?

My guess: the dream is urging me, "Even if you have to play on uneven ground… Even if you have to play at the steel firm you once owned… Even if you have to take a lesson when it's raining: make sure that you do it! That's how important it is for you to get back to golf!"

Frankly, I wouldn't have figured it's that crucial— but often one facet begun (such as restarting golf) can help the rest of us improve beyond what we might think.

Giving the Instinctive Force—the Force which covers all aspects of the physical— fresh activities can not only benefit the Instinctive but can also lead to sure improvements in the other Forces.

Watch for any new ideas. If you have a dream that brings up something that you've not ever done— say, playing the piano, taking guitar lessons, starting to paint— whatever you have a dream of— regard it eagerly, and consider it well— because tackling new themes in life can have amazing links to the rest of your self that allows more of you to build ever higher in your life's goal to be thriving.

And new habits can turn your life from being open to other people's smoking to being firm against that fate.

*   *   *   *

Here's last night's second dream that I'd like to review. Again, it has to do with golf.

Dream #2: 'I am standing with some golfers, and they're asking me to drive a golf ball at a tall white post that's maybe a hundred feet away. They're acting like I'm not going to come close to hitting it. I strike the ball with the proper club, and we all watch as the ball sails (straight as an arrow) towards the post, and then hits it at dead center. Everyone gasps in surprise. No one says a word to me—as one of them walks slowly to pick up the ball. I just stand there as bewildered as the rest of them.'

What's my experience with last night's second dream?

Of course, I am greatly amazed. It's the kind of shot I wouldn't bet I could make; and my image of myself in playing golf is far from serene self-confidence.

Yet here I thought: 'I hit that post!'

How does this dream improve the Force I'm working on?

You may not think it means this much— but in my own

mind the dream is saying, "Don't think you can't play golf with your slight skill. Start visualizing the kind of shot you made as well as the shots you'll make on all parts of the golf course... maybe your game will improve."

Dreams can help take us to new heights.

Try to believe that what I am showing you here will work for you just as you are.

The dream source that I have belongs to you as well— and will serve you as it serves me.

YOUR GOALS: TO BE SMOKE-FREE AND STRIVE TO BE THRIVING

DAY#44—TUESDAY—THE SEXUAL FORCE

IMPROVE YOUR SEXUAL FORCE THROUGH DREAMS—TO ACHIEVE YOUR GOALS!

WRITTEN UP DREAMS	*JOTTED DOWN DREAMS*

DAILY QUESTIONS TO ASK EACH OF THE DREAMS YOU HAVE:

#1.) WHAT'S MY EXPERIENCE WITH THIS DREAM FROM LAST NIGHT?

#2.) HOW DOES THIS DREAM IMPROVE THE FORCE I'M WORKING ON?

DAY FORTY-FOUR—TUESDAY—THE SEXUAL FORCE

Here's a mysterious dream that filled me with awe. See If you can understand why.

*   *   *   *

Dream #1: 'There's a situation where someone translated something into his own language from a language once not so familiar to him. The translation was no mean task. He worked hard to do it; and it was good enough to share with folks and charge for it.'

What's my experience with this sole dream last night?

I'm excited, pondering that this dream communicates in an almost hidden fashion something I've accomplished.

> Is it not strange how a resource that most folks "don't-know where-it-is" or "how-it-works" can send out a message that thrills me to the bone?

Maybe what I say makes no sense?

I am talking about a phenomenon that has baffled men and women as long as human beings have walked upon the earth.

Some folks have called dreams nothing but rubbish, which comes from our mind cleaning itself out. Others think they're disjointed sparks of mischief, which no one can ever rely on.

Yet, here we see a dream calmly communicating that someone has been able to translate his language into another language, and then to share what he's found with other folks.

What does that mean? I take it to mean that --from a fair amount of toil over the course of some years-- I'm gratefully able to share with you a means of translating your dreams with a plan that can help you steer clear of smoking and strive to live a life that is thriving.

"That is all well and good, and understandable-- but why focus on us?" You ask.

I have focused on ninth graders because-- with you in your

present stage of schooling-- you might have the freshest chance of understanding the method I am proposing: to start to use your dreams to accomplish your goals.

I have taken the liberty of choosing two goals for you to start engaging. Once you've got those two in your grasp, you are certainly free to continue with goals that you want to achieve as well.

How does this dream improve the Force I'm working on? (Today's Force is the Sexual.)

Now it would be easy to scoff at the effort of trying to see how this dream improves the Sexual Force that I'm working on. After all, where in last night's dream are there any signs or symbols of that one Force?

On the face of it, there are not. But one of the offshoots of this method is to try and tease from dreams whatever hints one can develop. By doing so we start to enlarge the scope of thinking that we're capable of.

So let's see what we find.

Is not sex a kind of language? Do we not often find how understanding that language is a challenge for us?

Isn't the key to a healthy sex life finding how to use sex for our own growth?

If we are baffled by the sexual surge of energy that teems within us— not nearly knowing what's the best way of handling it—might we not find ourselves shoved into all sorts of grief and lifespans of trouble?

So is not this dream revealing: that it's up to us to translate that sex-language (which is not words but energy) into our own language where we can deal with it?

Our translated language may be slightly different from the next man or woman. That's testament to its vision.

What's important for us --as we strive in our lives— is to

translate the language of sex into a language that we'll truly thrive by..

…As with sharing dreams, we can share this newfound language with others as it may be proper to do.

As to charging for it, there should be a charge for sharing in sex…but not money so much as need to receive a sincere sharing from another with that special slice of ourselves.

Then, too, it might be that our translation of the language of sex into our own language may not always require that we share our language with another soul.

Like the soul who writes words of poetry or prose for the earnest enjoyment of oneself, so it may be with the language of sex.

A thriving life may certainly encompass one who keeps his/her language private.

The key's how one thrives with one's best.

…Choosing this moment to branch off to another aspect of your comprehension-- often the best time to review how you're doing is when you have only one dream or maybe none at all to deal with on one day. It is then that you might care to turn back to the many numbers of days and see what achievements you have enjoyed--reviewing your dreams and your improvements from them.

Some of you may have gained insights that have made all of your efforts doubly worthwhile. Others may feel left out—searching….

It's one of those tough things in life to get hold of: that worthy goals are not easy for everyone to gain. Yet, often the person who refuses defeat winds up with more prizes than one who gains goals easily.

So: remember how you may have suffered several falls and scrapes when you first tried riding a bike? Hopefully, an experienced person stood near, encouraging you to keep on—giving you the will to never give up. So, too, I stand by you—giving you sound and true pep talks.

Again, as I mentioned before, you'll do me the honor of a call, e-mail or letter—commenting or asking me anything. that you have had trouble grasping.

Below is a list of ways you can contact me. I will do my best to help you.

e-mail: humbleracts@aol.com
phone: 314-574-7681
address: humbler acts/ 900 south hanley road/ unit 1-e/ clayton, mo 63105/ usa

Thank you for your pursuit of the goals outlined here.

Thank you for your continuous determination to benefit from the way dreams can be used to help you thrive.

YOUR GOALS: TO BE SMOKE-FREE AND STRIVE TO BE THRIVING

DAY#45—WEDNESDAY—THE MOVING FORCE

IMPROVE YOUR MOVING FORCE THROUGH DREAMS—TO ACHIEVE YOUR GOALS!

WRITTEN UP DREAMS	*JOTTED DOWN DREAMS*

DAILY QUESTIONS TO ASK EACH OF THE DREAMS YOU HAVE:

#1.) WHAT'S MY EXPERIENCE WITH THIS DREAM FROM LAST NIGHT?

#2.) HOW DOES THIS DREAM IMPROVE THE FORCE I'M WORKING ON?

DAY FORTY- FIVE—WEDNESDAY—THE MOVING FORCE

Here ae two short dreams that I encountered last night. Short dreams like these have value, too.

   *   *   *   *

Dream #1: 'I dreamed my alarm clock could hardly be heard as it began to go off nearby.'

What's my experience with this first dream last night?

Barely hearing an alarm could mean one is sleep-deprived— and determined not to be awakened by an alarm.

How does this dream improve the Force I'm working on? (The Moving Force.)

My guess is it's just reminding me that whether or not I can help lack of sleep, the first price I pay is the pain I have in getting myself up.

The second price-- the dream implies: is how disastrous it is for overall growth in not getting much sleep each night.

So many of us stay up late and then have to get up early; and the result is that our overall life of thriving suffers.

It can surely be told that with lack of sleep the patterns of natural growth— which we all should have as we mature-- are greatly affected in a negative way.

It's also true that when you aren't getting enough shuteye you'll likely remember a lot less dreams-- as shown above.

Not getting enough sleep makes us into losers-- in that our minds are not able to fully concentrate on any dreams we have.

So if you have been trying to adapt yourself to this primer and engage dreams, your lack of sleep may shortchange you.

Everyone seems to ask, "How much sleep should we get?"

First you need to value your sleep. Conventional wisdom then prescribes: sleep eight hours. At your age that's a minimum.

I'm sure many will say, "How can I sleep eight hours—with all the great late-night TV keeping me awake late!" Well, why not devise a way you'll tape shows and watch them at another time of day that won't interfere with the amount of sleep you should get?

Whatever value you assign to late TV should soon become irrelevant when compared to what you'll gain from engaging dreams.

Another point: ninth graders may feel that lack of money keeps them from enjoying themselves --as they see, hear or know others with wherewithals a lot richer than theirs.

But even the wealthiest of all the people you see or read about may not be privy to what you now know. For, deep within your selves may lie the hidden wealth that dreams hold ;and all you have to do is copy the steps outlined in this primer.

…So whatever is keeping you in your lack of sleep phase cannot be compared with the dreams you'll get with enough sleep.

Sleep, dreaming, and thriving may fill one big package.

William Shakespeare once composed: "To sleep perchance to dream." And I'd like to fashion it further: 'To dream, perchance to be.'

*   *   *   *

Here is the next dream from last night.

Dream #2:'I'm being introduced to exercises out at a golf club. There were a bunch of them I was doing. (Was the purpose of this to help improve how I'm playing?)'

What's my experience with last night's second dream?

It had never occurred to me there were exercises for helping my golf game.

I'd been thinking of getting a trainer to help get my balance and strength back from the normal loss of both due to my late operation; but I had not thought of seeing what the exercises might be that could also help me play better golf.

How does this dream improve the Force I am now working on?

Some of you may pooh-pooh what I'm going to say to you, but the truth is that the slightest of dreams can help us learn something we've not thought of—and in so learning it, life becomes more thriving.

If you'll recall how glad you might have become over the tiniest things in life, you will soon note that often your days are specially blessed with a bit of advice--a fresh action—a new feeling--the dawning of something that opens your eyes wide in gratitude: and it boosts you.

We often yearn for stuff in superficial ways that might never satisfy us.

Habitually, we tend to overlook how small gifts in life—that could help us-- are more often within our grasp as we dream them.

Even at my older age I marvel at how often I'm refreshed day by day with the knowledge that dreams provide.

Imagine how much more you can gain at your age from starting to recall your dreams-- and experiencing them the best way you can and then asking yourself how they can keep you from smoking and help you improve your life so that it becomes thriving.

Now here's the answer to the question: how did the second dream last night improve the Force I am working on? (It is the Moving Force.)

Reluctant as I was to look: I checked the Internet, and found a number of sites that showed five exercises that I could start using to improve my golf game.

I would never have guessed that such exercises were there

for me to start using.

Here is a typical instance of how we can engage a dream so that we are encouraged to improve our lives to be thriving. And the more we thrive in our lives, the further we stay from any temptation that beckons us to begin smoking.

YOUR GOALS: TO BE SMOKE-FREE AND STRIVE TO BE THRIVING

DAY#46 THURSDAY—THE FEELING FORCE

IMPROVE YOUR FEELING FORCE THROUGH DREAMS—TO ACHIEVE YOUR GOALS!

WRITTEN UP DREAMS	*JOTTED DOWN DREAMS*

DAILY QUESTIONS TO ASK EACH OF THE DREAMS YOU HAVE:

#1.) WHAT'S MY EXPERIENCE WITH THIS DREAM FROM LAST NIGHT?

#2.) HOW DOES THIS DREAM IMPROVE THE FORCE I'M WORKING ON?

DAY FORTY-SIX—THURSDAY—THE FEELING FORCE

Check out this first dream that I encountered last night. What it says should encourage you.

      *   *   *   *

Dream #1: 'Somebody was raising a flag in somebody's honor. I was with a young son. The flag pole stood quite tall—with the flag just starting to go up to a certain height.'

What's my experience with this first dream last night?

…Another short dream… but it left me feeling that some growth has been made in the time you and I have been together.

So the flag we see there is raised in our honor— on our behalf— for what we've done.

What is it that we've done? We've made a start in this primer –learning how to use dreams.

We've started to see how the purpose of dreams is to improve our Seven Forces; and-- while improving them— we've started preparing our minds and hearts to live thriving lives and keep from smoking.

Now, that flagpole is tall. And since there's still work yet to do-- the flag's not going all the way to the top yet.

I surmise the boy next to me may have represented all of you as a group.

How does this dream improve the Force that I am working on?

It publicized to me that our work has not been in vain—that hopefully each of you is doing your part to learn how to keep from smoking as well as starting to live a life that's thriving.

Each time dreams grant us glimpses of honor and fresh praise… they encourage us to keep improving and finding new ways. .

      *   *   *   *

Here is the second dream that I noted last night. It's a bit long but stay through it.

Dream #2: 'I talk with a girl friend from way back in my youth. It was May the first. And in the dream it was her birthday. A group was gathering someplace nearby, and we all got in cars and were driving there. An old friend asks how to handle the cash. Do we show it as cash or not? When I tried to answer, he smiled and tapped me on the chest and said, "C'mon, you know I don't care!" Then he talked of all the small streets that had auto repairs on them as if all these places were now hopelessly mired in poverty. Before—as I talked with my old girlfriend—she looked so different from her vibrant self of so many years past. Nevertheless, I was quite fascinated seeing and talking with her again. A guy came up to ask her something; and I stepped aside so he could. Then she put a cigarette in her mouth and swallowed it—while others were getting cigarettes (I guess before they left for the meeting); and I actually was tempted to steal one—but didn't.'

What's my experience with last night's second dream?

Remembering that old girlfriend evoked feelings of how gentle life was back then. It was just the two of us and not much to trouble with.

The girl in this dream was someone whom I liked very much-- though it was puppy love, and was soon replaced by ambition that detached us.

Yet the dream ushered in sentiment that was key to newfound bliss.

Certainly, there's no turning backward to those days— except in dreams.

Regrettably, her destiny darkened when she latched on to a smoking habit.

When she swallowed that cigarette, I was appalled—sensing her devouring was no more stupid than her smoking it.

When we were young sweethearts, she hadn't smoked one yet.

Perhaps her act in the dream was like her saying "I'm not good for you anymore!"

Regarding the question my friend asked in the dream: was he indifferent in that he didn't' care what was the right way to handle feelings…whether we should express them or hide them inside our chest?

I believe dreams teach us we should express feelings. And maybe that's what I needed to be more aware of-- while he didn't much care.

Most folks don't care? This dream says, "Care."

How does this dream improve the Force I'm working on?

It's all about handling feelings. So many get buried and are never expressed.

Dreams help us to address feelings.

There are many of us who enact decent deeds, yet the feeling side of us has been suppressed and smothered with our teenage coolness

…And those who smoke further mask their feelings by stuffing them with the smoke they inhale.

In this dream, my old friend does show emotion when he talks of the car repairmen who are stuck in their poverty.

As I'm writing this I am reminded that I mentioned in past pages how "car' in dreams may signify: "mechanism of will".

So here are some car mechanics who tinker on their "wills" rather than improve them.

Tinkering won't bring improvement.

Once we can really get to the heart of feelings --and that's a chore for all of us-- we will have the use of one of the greatest of human Forces that now exists. Traditionally, few have known how to use that.

I propose to you that your dreams can guide you quite subtly towards dealing with feelings.

Dreams are the tools that can do that.

*   *   *   *

Here is the third dream that I wrote down from last night. It's a ticklish thought to observe.

Dream #3: 'I recall a dream where I'm talking with a guy, who's telling me no one can say a thing of anyone without getting into trouble. I say, 'It does seem true. But people just don't stand being hurt. They rise up—angry—and try to control it.'

What's my experience with this third dream last night?

Often in dreams we find ourselves thinking thoughts that we might not have thought of before.

It's almost as if dreams plug the holes of unawareness that line our outer selves.

We go around using language to brief others without ever considering that what we say may cause trouble.

Wouldn't our lives be more thriving if we took care to hold back words that hurt others?

Dreams can help us become more conscious of the fine line between not sharing feelings and sharing them to the detriment of others.

How does this dream improve the Force that I am working on?

Sometimes we need to be super careful when we review the dreams we have written down. For instance-- in the above shown dream-- we read that "No one can say a thing of someone without getting into trouble." "Of" is the key word to understand what we should heed from the dream.

Why is that so? Because when we say something "of" people, we are talking about the whole of them— their very selves. No one cares to have his or her very self hurt.

But saying a thing TO people carries a lot less risk in terms of hurting them. They might even listen to you!

We may talk about the behavior or actions of certain folks but never them. Their actions are not them.

I think actions can be talked about but not character. At least that's the message that comes to me right now.

As I've implied, my dreams are mine. What they help me see may just not work for you now. What you dream will be what you need. My dreams may start you off…but then you go to yours.

As we wind down this fifty day dream primer, I hope you are getting true value from your efforts with what I've shown.

If events or crises have prevented you from spending time with this dream primer, please do not feel that your opportunity is lost. You can start over again.

There are few ninth graders who have ever achieved much without pain from first efforts. You may look at someone out there who reached success… and then wander behind the scenes of his or her early life and find all had their share of setbacks before success.

One might even say that without setbacks there can be no success---in that setbacks are the steps one takes to produce future success.

…So always count yourself, "Still in!"

YOUR GOALS: TO BE SMOKE-FREE AND STRIVE TO BE THRIVING

DAY#47 FRIDAY—THE THINKING FORCE

IMPROVE YOUR THINKING FORCE THROUGH DREAMS—TO ACHIEVE YOUR GOALS!

WRITTEN UP DREAMS	*JOTTED DOWN DREAMS*

DAILY QUESTIONS TO ASK EACH OF THE DREAMS YOU HAVE:

#1.) WHAT'S MY EXPERIENCE WITH THIS DREAM FROM LAST NIGHT?

#2.) HOW DOES THIS DREAM IMPROVE THE FORCE I'M WORKING ON?

DAY FORTY-SEVEN—FRIDAY—THE THINKING FORCE

I wanted first to talk about one key phrase that appeared in both my dreams last night.

"Expanded metal" is the key phrase; and I hope my discussion will throw apt light on the importance of seeing a meaning in a key phrase that happens to come from another phrase that has a similar sound.

Here are the two dreams with that phrase:

*   *   *   *

Dream #1:'Someone was telling us about the various sizes of a well-known product—"expanded metal"—which happens to be the small opening stuff used for outdoor furniture. We saw the various cut-to-length sizes afloat on the water.'

Dream #2: 'There was an issue with expanded metal (Could it be "mettle?) where we're sending over to a guy a certain size with a style (called flat), and then seriously worry that what we are sending would not work. We called up the guy and only when we insisted he think about what we sent and about what he actually was going to need that it finally dawned on him it's not quite what he needed. Then…once he began to understand more clearly, he thought he could use what we sent. (Only after going back and forth did I realize –after waking up—that in order to get something out of the dream I had to take the sound "expanded metal" and make it "expanded METTLE"— which meant something about ability to cope well with difficulties.)'

What's my experience with this dream-phrase last night?

Until I hit upon the word "mettle"-- for expanded "metal"—I was floating on water with no direction.

Here is an example where the word with the same sound needs to be given credence.

First let me clarify how "mettle" improves us. If you possess "mettle", you are 'a person who has the ability to cope well with tough things or to face a taxing situation in a spirited

[178]

and resilient way.'

...And "expanded" lends meaning to something (as the Thinking Force) that has been enlarged from what it was.

So now that we have learned how important this phrase is (Once we've used it with "mettle"), let's go back to what we ask when we deal with dreams.

Recall the first question we ask?

What's my experience with this first dream last night?

Frankly, without the word "mettle"-- expanded metal was laying in the water without any purpose to it.

How does this dream improve the Force I'm working on?

If we are not wary, we can waste our "mettle" floating around without purpose.

Dreams can help us by revealing that we are loafing when we really should not be…

Metal, that's been expanded, should be used for furniture; and "expanded mettle" should be used on worthwhile projects.

What's my experience with last night's second dream?

Here I'm perplexed—but shall presume that whoever we are giving the "mettle" to realized that it wasn't quite what he thought he needed…though he may still use it.

How does this dream improve the Force that I am working on?

"We"—that is I—cannot give you "mettle" for your own use… You really need to take note from your own dreams what "mettle" you'll need… Not that what I am giving you has no value at all for you…

For example, it may help you: know what is right for you— intellectually— And you might say, "That's pretty cool."

But "mettle" will have to develop well within you to help meet your own needs now.

      *   *   *   *

Here is the third dream that I wrote down from last night. (I hope new thought will come from it.)

Dream #3: 'I'm sharing a living quarter with some guys. I am awakened because of some matter and struggle to get myself dressed. At first I throw on a plain bathrobe to rush to the place that is needing me now. No! That won't do. Walking outside in a bathrobe wouldn't look right. So I throw on a pair of shorts—and a shirt—totally contrasting in colors and style. I'm ready to leave now…Also a huge amount of water pours in from a window top—why?—we can't understand—Also a guy is going to drive to some area but then imposes on me to walk there.'

With a dream like this, it would be easy to throw in the towel and simply give up. But calmly stay with the way I've been showing you.

The following question calms us:

What's my experience with this third dream last night?

The dream has cast me in a role that's far from where I am (at least in my real life).

But the dream wants me in this role…

…Thus maybe the role is instructive enough that I'll grasp something that improves me.

Nothing normal is shown. I don't have my own home. There's no semblance of life control.

I get awakened by something that forces me to tend to it. There is no time to get properly dressed (something I like to do). Then I witness a window's flood-- over which I'm helpless-- and then some guy forces me to walk while he goes by car.

All of the above shows a life that's lost control.

How does this dream improve the Force I am now working on? (It is the Thinking Force.)

How fragile is the life I live. How oppressive it would be to wind up like this poor fellow shown here in this dream!

I may feel that I am well-grounded-- as I live-- but this dream is telling me "No!"

How does "No!" improve me? It lets me know that life can suddenly upend my ease.

For one who lives in a nice condo with his wife, circumstances could in some way turn me into a guy sharing strangers' quarters and suffering suspended sleep.

Dreams can show us the way to live to be thriving. Dreams can also remind us to never take for granted the good fortune we've gained..

Many a soul has found itself thrown off a normal course-- thanks to a bad lifestyle… And no soul can swear it's immune.

With a human being, anything's possible: anything, bad; anything, good.

As ninth graders your task might be to guard against uncertainty in your life by resolving through your dreams to strive for a thriving existence that starts out smoke-free.

YOUR GOALS: TO BE SMOKE-FREE AND STRIVE TO BE THRIVING

DAY#48 SATURDAY—THE HIGHER FEELING FORCE

IMPROVE YOUR HIGHER FEELING FORCE THROUGH DREAMS—TO ACHIEVE YOUR GOALS!

WRITTEN UP DREAMS	*JOTTED DOWN DREAMS*

DAILY QUESTIONS TO ASK EACH OF THE DREAMS YOU HAVE:

#1.) WHAT'S MY EXPERIENCE WITH THIS DREAM FROM LAST NIGHT?

#2.) HOW DOES THIS DREAM IMPROVE THE FORCE I'M WORKING ON?

DAY FORTY-EIGHT—SATURDAY—THE HIGHER FEELING FORCE

Here's an interesting dream I wrote down last night. It might almost be magical.

*   *   *   *

Dream #1:'There was a dream that had some kind of glittering mirror-like bowl, and it came with a saying: LOOK UPON HERE FIRST—BEFORE WINNING THERE. It seemed that a small mirror could be used in place of the bowl. A mystery surrounded the way the bowl worked.'

What's my experience with this first dream last night.

That bowl has a breathtaking breadth. Its cut-glass appears to be exceedingly rare...

I am intrigued by its saying. It reminded me of the stories that are told about people using mirrors in order to seal their good fortune with an oath: "Mirror, Mirror On The Wall", etc.

The thought of just having a small mirror for that precise purpose struck my fancy.

How does this dream improve the Force I'm working on? (It's the Higher Feeling Force, now.)

I have no assurance that one's reflection in a mirror stamps a response on the Higher Feeling Force— so that the saying "LOOK UPON HERE FIRST-- BEFORE WINNING THERE" would drive one to thrive.

But as doctors mostly tell-- when asked of a nutrient's health claims-- "Well, it can't hurt!"...

So holding up a small mirror to one's face and stating the above mentioned words-- as one gets ready for another day-- probably won't add more wins to one's life.

...But then one never knows... Perhaps this weird ritual has properties that we, mere mortals, can't discern-- and does manage in some bizarre way to keep us safe from harm and instill confidence in all the aims we take that day.

Here is the second dream that I wrote down last night. (Cigarettes are the subject here:)

Dream #2: 'I had taken care of getting beige sweaters for everyone, and took the bunch of them inside—as we got together after a drive to a friend's house. Someone asked how a cigarette was and then said: "One guy said his was cockeyed." I then thank the driver for the good job he had done getting us safely to where we were going.'

What's my experience with last night's second dream?

My favorite color is beige. But I don't don sweaters; I only wear jackets.

How strange to stick my favorite color on sweaters that I'd never choose to wear. It's almost like relishing my role of admonishing ninth graders not to smoke. One thing I like; one thing I don't.

…So when one guy reports that another guy says, "His cigarette was cockeyed", I have to believe that at least one guy gets my point.

If one dreams that cigarettes are "absurd …impractical", such pronouncements may have more impact than preachers' preaching.

How does this dream improve the Force I'm working on?

In my heart I know that smoking is most likely the worst anti-health behavior that ninth graders can undertake.. That's why part of this book's dedicated to the goal of keep- Ing ninth graders from taking up cigarettes.

My hope is that through my own dreams as well as through dreams of the ninth graders, themselves, resounding reasons will be brought to mind that will show them --more assertively than books, slogans or folks' words-- never ever to start smoking.

    *   *   *   *

Here is the third dream that I wrote down from last night. (Sometimes a dream gives us a fit.)

Dream #3: 'A group of us are in the basement of my house (in the dream). One guy has a fake snake-like figure with a man's face and throws it at another man in playfulness. I try to make sure that all are behaving well. As some question the whereabouts of an absent fellow, he's suddenly standing in front of us with a black eye.'

What's my experience with this third dream last night?

I'm the host, but seemingly not keeping much order here. First, one guy childishly bothers a guy with a fake snake. Then a guy appears with a black eye, which has got to get people asking, "How's that?"

How does this dream improve the Force I'm working on? (We're still on the Higher Feeling.)

Warning: when we think a dream isn't helping us, we need to pause and query more:

Am I responsible for other folks' conduct? It's my house, But do I rule folks?

I am no one's ruler… The minute I think that… I am losing my fair focus, which should be on how I'll strive to be more thriving.

There's nothing like sustaining a sense of humor in all the striving that we do.

Just when we think we are in charge, a guy throws a fake snake with a guy's face on it— surely about as silly an action as one could take.

…And the guy with the black eye?… He just lost a fight or came out of it with a black badge of mischief-making.

So, improving this Higher Force comes down to becoming aware that just when we might feel we are making headway in our goal to live a life that is thriving, life causes us to suffer a bit with fuss inside of us or fuss outside of us.

You've heard the phrase: "Grin and bear it"? Well, that's sort of what we have to do at such times.

Life does not step aside when we are striving to thrive more. On the contrary, we might find ourselves confronting a lot of horseplay that we have no way to control.

My advice is: just hang in there.

Dreams can help us withstand all the disappointments that otherwise might dismay us.

    *   *   *   *

Here is another dream that I wrote down last night. (It's very short and to the point.)

Dream #4: 'I pull my car forwards in a parking space. As I apply the brakes, the car slides on hardly- noticed ice— until the entire car goes slightly beyond the space.'

What's my experience with this fourth dream last night?

Surprise? Surprise! No one gets hurt, but it's a wake-up call telling me: I may be driving safely, but I'm not safe... Other things intercede that make bad things happen.

Whoever we are, whatever we've done, none of us in cars can ever escape the fact that we're responsible.

When we have such a dream, it might be laying the foundation for avoiding an accident of some sort.

We must never forget our well-being is what dreams teach.

I can't state they predict the future, but dreams may detect a kind of behavior that we are guilty of, that can presage a form of accident that could come soon.

    •   *   *   *

Here is the fifth dream that I wrote down from last night. (It's a promise I hope is kept.).

Dream #5: 'When I bathe you—you do not look like the same child.'

What's my experience with this fifth dream last night?

Nothing could be sweeter than a dream that paints a picture of a freshly bathed child.

Isn't that the sort of relief we would all cherish as we seek a thriving life?

I think dreams can do that for us.

No matter how we spurn our lifestyles right now, a "dream's bathing" can refresh anew.

How does this dream improve the Force I'm working on?

Dreams do bathe us. They can drive us through a dream-wringer, too! Nevertheless, dreams grant us new insights that make us glow.

I guess it's safe to say: over time we won't look or feel or think like the same child.

"You're looking different…What are you doing now?" may be a close ally's comment.

…'Something is not the same in the way you react to the outside world you live in.'

Dreams are not a quick-fix. Dreams may not make you rich. You're not going to rule others. But others may respect you in different ways.

You can keep your change a secret or you may share your new interest in your dreams.

But dreams aren't for everybody. So be careful with whom you dare start to share dreams.

Some people are put off by dreams. You can mostly tell that by the cast of their face. If it's puzzled, change the subject. If it is quite eager, try one step at a time.

It may surprise you who could be interested in your pursuit of learning dreams.

Friendships may be drawn much closer when two or more become fascinated with the exploration of dream thriving..

•   *   *   *

Here is the last dream that I wrote down from last night. (Here again we see a warning.)

Dream #6: 'An old school chum of mine tells me he left his car at my place of business and nervously joked he hoped it was still there. It was night time, and I happened to go down and see other cars—but not his. I entered the steel warehouse and saw that the TV was still on. I walked over to shut it off but was thrown off balance when a voice was heard coming from the TV saying my first name. Then I heard someone banging on the front door. Who could that be—so late? I froze—confused what I should do.'

What's my experience with this sixth dream last night?

Just typing up this dream scares me. It's like the beginning of a mystery tale. I'm not much for frightening tales. Life is scary enough without conjuring them. Why look for more to frighten us?

How does this dream improve the Force I'm working on?

Can you see where I am blindly exposing myself to needless kinds of danger?

My business is not to go to a warehouse at night that can give me the creeps.

I used to work down there at night, and I thank the Lord that nothing ever happened—but that was luck. The odds were there for me to have problems that I needn't have had.

All of us should sense deep down that holding ourselves in harm's way is totally dumb.

We should honor the fact we live and take great care that we stay far from losing life.

There is plenty of wonderment in learning all that life has for us to thrive with.

If we are bored with how we live, now is a perfect time to recognize that dreams will wisely point us toward new ways that will swiftly "un-bore" us and stimulate, too.

As we become better informed about how dreams improve our chances to avoid the world's hazards, so we become a lot better prepared for the blessings of life-- through relaxing and studying dreams..

YOUR GOALS: TO BE SMOKE-FREE AND STRIVE TO BE THRIVING

DAY#49 SUNDAY—THE HIGHER THINKING FORCE

IMPROVE YOUR HIGHER THINKING FORCE THROUGH DREAMS—TO ACHIEVE YOUR GOALS!

WRITTEN UP DREAMS	JOTTED DOWN DREAMS

DAILY QUESTIONS TO ASK EACH OF THE DREAMS YOU HAVE:

#1.) WHAT'S MY EXPERIENCE WITH THIS DREAM FROM LAST NIGHT?

#2.) HOW DOES THIS DREAM IMPROVE THE FORCE I'M WORKING ON?

DAY FORTY-NINE—SUNDAY—THE HIGHER THINKING FORCE

Here's the initial dream I wrote down from last night. (Eye-opening--to say the least.)

*   *   *   *

Dream #1:'My mother comes into my office consumed with hysteria and grabs the phone out of my hands. I then throw a glass of water towards her, and it shatters against the wall. Tiny pieces of glass rain down upon the floor as she walks out.'

What's my experience with this first dream last night?

My mom never bore this brand of mania while she lived; and she never harassed me during her long one hundred years of life..

Yet the spirit I carry of her has been sorely bent out of shape by the Higher Thinking Force I am now fostering.

By the way: her spirit does not have anything to do with the fact she's deceased. The spirit I'm referring to is simply a construct I have of her from life.

Thanks to drama in this dream, I'm not backing down on what I'm currently doing… even if she is my mother.

We can say what we want about a son tossing a glass filled with water past his mother—but my sense is--from her implying I'm a phony—I am obliged to protest with broken glass-- thereby denying her authority to divert me.

How does this dream improve the Force I'm working on?

The Higher Force-- I'm dealing with-- requires a belief that there is such a Force. From the above-mentioned dream, it strikes me my mother was no great believer in this Force. I am, so the dream drove me to defend myself on behalf of this Force.

Surely, I had not ever mused my mom would make a fuss… Hence my defense strengthens my resolve.

I bring all this up in the hope you will see how a dream can bring to mind something that may never have been consciously thought of— but which needs to be known—in order to thrive even more.

When we have fierce dreams like the one above, often we need to take time perusing and thinking about it. I caution you on this: if dreams make you terribly tied to anxieties that you've a hard time handling, don't let them harm unheeded: HALT!

I would not wish any of you ninth graders to confront dreaming that disturbs you to a point where you are frightfully uneasy.

"Demons" may be long locked up in your past; and if dreams of them enter consciousness -- where they become unbearable-- then I would stay away from encountering them.

My hope is that you will truly improve your life through the striving that you're doing— but if you find your life's going contrary to your goals— because your dreams are so stern and stressful—stop for a while.

I believe that even dire dreams have a purpose to help improve at least one Force.

Gradually over time you may toughen up to where you will deal with demons.

Time is a great healer--even healing demons.

I believe, too, that –however you may flag or fail with the goals we've set herein-- love is the thing that will save you.

  *   *   *   *

Here is the second dream that I had this past night. (This dream holds the key with "word play".)

Dream #2:: "There had also been a dream where a doctor is advising me to double up on the daily dosage of Cialis I was taking—but just for this one night.'

What's my experience with last night's second dream?

In this dream, I sensed that doubling up would be dangerous, so I was surprised to hear the doctor come up with that. I couldn't see how I could go with his advice.

The Cialis I've been taking seems to be kicking in normally—as far as giving me the desired results.

But the doctor seems to have something else in mind.

Now for a pause: what you've just read is a valiant attempt to experience what I found in the above shown dream.

In writing about it, I've been forced to stick with the actual content of the dream. But sometimes in my adhering to content, I've found that I have not gotten a sense of the essence of what the dream's saying.

That's when the next question helps me dig a little deeper and see where the dream goes.

Let us see where it heads from here.

How does this dream improve the Force I'm working on?

The truth is not always in dreams...Or at least not in dreams that narrate certain facts.

Yet rest assured the truth will out. But sometimes truth's disguised in fanciful fashion.

So how is truth disguised right here?

To me, it's disguised in the sound of Cialis as it becomes SEE ALL (that) IS.

The Higher Thinking is where one SEES ALL (that) IS. It's the top spot of our being.

It is only after I went through this second phase of dream work --as I've shown you-- that I received a fresh shot of awareness—through my quite sudden glimpsing that the word Cialis held the key with: SEE ALL (that) IS-- which stamped the dream strongly in mind.

You as a spectator to this "word play" may pan it as mental toying around with meaning, but when you have your own dreams—as I hope you have or will have real soon—you'll find "word play" helps you very positively in enhancing your goals-- as you begin to have greater awareness of dreams' power.

The more you dream, the more you'll be.

*   *   *   *

Here's the third and final dream I wrote down last night.
(It's a scene that truly startles.)

Dream #3: 'I dream of a piece of furniture that was in the entrance hall of the house I grew up in. The only thing different in its construction was that in the dream you could put a bag full of trash through the top of it—once you took off a portion of the top. And there was a place inside where the trash bag settled. You couldn't tell from the outside that this lovely furniture piece held trash. As I put the bag in there, I noticed Mother doing some place setting in the dining room quite nearby.'

What's my experience with this third dream last night?

I'm quite young in this dream; and I see myself as a kid dutifully stashing trash in a piece of furniture.

This weird scene features so pathetically how I must have been raised without my consciously knowing it. How strange to see it then.

And there's Mother-- minding me as I execute my chore— while she makes sure all seems *en tout* when we sit down to dine.

How does this dream improve the Force I'm working on?

Anytime we can discern truth that helps explain our past, we start building ourselves into adults with more future. .

It's been proven time and again that regardless of what our past has been, we can learn ways to deal with it and rise to greater heights.

Ninth graders may not have learned this. Some get suckered into miserable victimized mindsets—though their dreams could help them become more solidly prepared (freed from excuse) to strive in a thriving manner. We can never change our past, but if we perceive meddle-some things impacting us, we'll move past them in a more positive manner.

It's the present we inhabit. We can only dwell there—by making sure we don't suffer stuff that inhibits us.

Dreams help us to improve and thrive in the present—by getting us beyond our past:

The past needn't cripple—regardless what it was—while dreams give us fresh breathing space for skipping beyond it.

You're at an age in life when your past is really recent—so you've got a stronger chance of understanding it and quickly getting past it.

Let me add that I am not a professional practitioner of mind science; and I don't want you to worry you have to be.

It doesn't take "education" to learn from your own dreams how to thrive wholesomely..

Your dreams are your dreams; and your goals of keeping from smoking and striving towards thriving can be reached through your own efforts.

It is so important to value all of you—your past and your present and your future. No one takes that from you-- as long as your being stays connected to your spirit.

YOUR GOALS: TO BE SMOKE-FREE AND STRIVE TO BE THRIVING

DAY#50 MONDAY—THE INSTINCTIVE FORCE

IMPROVE YOUR INSTINCTIVE FORCE THROUGH DREAMS—TO ACHIEVE YOUR GOALS!

WRITTEN UP DREAMS	JOTTED DOWN DREAMS

DAILY QUESTIONS TO ASK EACH OF THE DREAMS YOU HAVE:

#1.) WHAT'S MY EXPERIENCE WITH THIS DREAM FROM LAST NIGHT?

#2.) HOW DOES THIS DREAM IMPROVE THE FORCE I'M WORKING ON?

DAY FIFTY—MONDAY—THE INSTINCTIVE FORCE

Here is the first of three dreams I wrote down last night. (Note how this first dream informed me.)

   *   *   *   *

Dream #1:"'How's this place different from others'?" someone asked. "It's a refuge here for women.'"

What's my experience with this first dream last night?

I learned something from what it said.

Although I have never consciously thought that this dream primer would be a refuge for women --as opposed to what it is for men-- I could see how this dream is right.

Women have always been known to be a lot more introspective with their feelings. Women, generally, have experienced a richer inner life than have men.

So I can readily admit this dream primer would be closer to what women seek than it would be for what men of all kinds seek.

But is it not possible that this dream primer could be a refuge for the side of men that is feminine, too? Could it not also be a refuge for men who have never had much of a chance to cultivate the side of themselves that has to do with inner feelings and thoughts?

What better way to start to liberate this part of themselves than to remember and use dreams to keep from smoking as well as to strive towards thriving with richer lives?

How does this dream improve the Force I'm working on? (Recall: it's the Instinctive Force.)

I--as well as any man participating in this primer—should be aware of the importance of striving towards becoming more feminine in our quest to build our Seven Forces more harmoniously--by using dreams for our self-growth.

It is easy for us—as men—to shrug off dreams and direct our minds and hearts towards more aggressive pursuits than focusing on dreams.

But we don't have to give up our masculinity by cultivating the side of us that is more feminine. We can grow on both sides--as we gain a foothold in the art of assaying dreams.

   *   *   *   *

Here, now, is the second dream I wrote down last night. (Sometimes one dream tracks another.)

Dream #2: 'I'm walking arm in arm with a woman and see lights on the stairs of a building in front of us. Each light brightens the bottom tread of the stairs. It's around Christmas.'

What's my experience with last night's second dream?

The structure seemed to be around seven stories in height. In sizing it up it, I thought the stories were the Seven Forces of informed steps we've been taking each week.

…And having found that dream work is a refuge for women (or for the feminine side of a man) I was guiding this person (as proxy for every ninth grader) towards the place she can call her own.

It seemed fitting that I would be doing this on the last day of our dream primer.

How does this dream improve the Force I'm working on?

I'm elated-- walking towards that seven story building with a woman in hand… I hope I've had some influence in guiding her towards the fulfillment of her dreams—represented by that building, which each participant attains in this dream work.

When we have a dream like this one, often we can bring to mind the picture of it in later days. Recalling it may give further strength in our striving to thrive more.

…All day long our thoughts are random; and occasionally, inserting in our mind a picture of this tall building may help keep us on track towards achieving our goals.

        *   *   *   *

Here is the third dream that I jotted down last night. (It's a little bit different.)

Dream #3: 'An ugly tooth that looks closer to a fang has the end of it—about an inch long—broken off from the main part. It's on a string that allows the small part of the fang to slide to the end that has become missing. I don't think it belongs to me.'

What's my experience with this third dream last night?

In such a dream it's logical to search for meaning in the midst of guessing what or whom the tooth may belong to.

Such a dream seems far from where we normally are.

It struck me the ugly tooth was a branch of science that has made the common man believe only professionals can assist him with dreams. That's not totally true but pretty close to what I've sensed.

I thought—maybe in some down-to-earth-way—I had broken off part of this tooth for people to regain their own power to use dreams.

How does this dream improve the Force that I am working on? (Again: the Instinctive.)

It reveals an image that can strengthen my resolve to keep on guiding people (primarily the ninth graders)— who in their youthful selves harbor seeds to show the world how to yield more thriving lives.

        *   *   *   *

Here is the fourth and last dream that I had last night. (It speaks about having patience.)

Dream #4: 'I happen to be at the dentist (not the one that I go to in my real life). I walk towards the dentist's chair— as my appointment time arrives—just as a woman is conversing with the dentist. Then I hear the other dentist call to the first—asking him if he has time for a quick story. Meanwhile, I turn and start back to a seat in the small room adjoining whence I'd walked and proceed to wait a bit more'

What's my experience with this fourth dream last night?

I'm a patient man; and the dream shows this feature in me. I wasn't always so.

Now I believe that one's time comes— not necessarily when one demands it to— but when the time is ripe... it comes. I know that's pretty vague, but it's the sense I have.

So though I did want to sit down and get started with what the dentist had to do, the delay did not anger me.

Who the woman is... and what the story's about...didn't seem to be important. The dream just showed what I have been forced to become.

How does this dream improve the Force that I am working on?

It just reinforces an attribute I acquired-- only after I had lived through many failures-- and found that the world's time table wasn't the same as mine.

I had to learn to wait. Waiting is not like giving up. Waiting simply means to never give up thriving Giving up means quitting thriving.

When youths refuse to smoke, they are agreeing to never turn their backs on thriving...

When youths start to smoke, that's when they give up thriving.

So determine to keep thriving.

    *   *   *   *

Now I'd like to review what you've been involved with: a dream primer of fifty days.

Firstly, you were given the task of joining your Seven Forces with the seven days of the week. So you ended up with these pairs:

Monday—the Instinctive Force
Tuesday—the Sexual Force
Wednesday—the Moving Force
Thursday—the Feeling Force
Friday—the Thinking Force
Saturday—the Higher Feeling Force
Sunday—the Higher Thinking Force

Next you were shown how you could build up these Seven Forces. Each of these Forces was going to be improved by the dreams that you have on each seventh day of the week.

A procedure was shown to you:

You would remind yourselves upon going to bed that you wanted to dream in ways that would improve the Force of the following day.

When the new day came, at some point you would look upon the dream(s) and query them thus: (after having written them up):

(1) What's my experience with this new dream I've had? And after you've expressed yourself, you would follow with the next (2.) How does this dream improve the Force I'm working on?

As time went on you would acquire enough strength to be able to tackle the two goals you agreed to :

(1) To always stay smoke-free

(2) To strive to thrive in life.

It is only from your working with your dreams—which in turn are meant to improve each of your Seven Forces—that you can build yourself to a point where you can withstand the all-round persistent peer pressure for smoking.

Each one of those Seven Forces can exert positive refusals for smoking. Thus, no Force lets you start smoking.

People can blow smoke in your face; yet you refuse. They

can offer you cigarettes or urge you to be cool; yet you will still refuse.

And along with your newfound strength to steer clear of smoking, you will be able to strive to thrive with a better life.

Ideas that you found in your numerous dreams may allow you to start on new ventures only now known. Even one or two can add to your life or well change it.

By going fifty days you've gone from slave-like lives to youths who have achieved freedom.

* * * *

In an ancient culture, folks called a certain time, THE JUBILEE.

And what was that?

The Jubilee was a fifty year period of time-- at the end of which slaves were given their freedom.

Imagine how they'd feel! Freedom at last! They tasted it. They celebrated it. Now their lives were their own… Just as your life has become yours.

Now I don't want you to get carried away and think freedom means disregard for others or negligence of your body or mind.

Far from that—you ought to have learned that real freedom means that you truly take yourself seriously. You recognize what a wholesome blessing you can become in life. You've succeeded in not smoking and have begun to see just how you really can strive in your life to be thriving.

* * * *

It's time for me to sign off. I've taken you as far as I can. You're on your own.

As I've said several times, let me hear from you with anything you'd care to say.

My cell: humbleracts@aol.com

My phone: 314-574-7681

My address: Humbler Acts, 900 South Hanley Road, Unit 1-E, Clayton, MO 63105, USA

Good luck, God speed to each of you!

Humbler Acts